GRO YOU POSITIVE MINDSET

Step-By-Step to Boost Positivity, Practice Positive Mindset Habits, Recognize Your Strengths, Change Your Life, and Achieve Success

Larin Carney

Table of Contents

CRAFTING AND ACHIEVING MEANINGFUL GOALS 143

INTRODUCTION

Of this, be sure: You do not find the happy life—
you make it. –Thomas Monson

A Happy Life

What does a happy life look like to you? Maybe it's owning a house overlooking the ocean with a breathtaking view—and you often picture yourself sitting on the porch in the evenings, sipping on a cup of chamomile tea while the cool breeze gently brushes your cheeks. It's quiet and serene, and all you can hear is the sound of the waves from the ocean. You think to yourself, "This is paradise."

Perhaps your idea of a happy life is raising your family in the countryside, surrounded by nature. You have a job that allows you to work from home, which gives you ample time to spend with your family, and you don't have to spend hours stuck in traffic driving to and from work.

We all have different ideas of what a happy life looks like. For some, it is achieving career success, finding a partner who loves and supports their dreams, or having a great relationship with their family. For others, it's about discovering inner peace and purpose in life and living each day with intention. Despite the differences in our goals, we all

1

desire to experience peace of mind in a world full of chaos and to feel a sense of fulfillment.

Speaking of chaos, life can be unpredictable at times. Maybe you're going through a difficult period in your life, or you're struggling to achieve your goals, and you're wondering if things will ever improve. I want you to know that you are not alone.

Everyone experiences challenges and setbacks in various aspects of their lives, such as relationships, finances, or work. When faced with adversity, it's easy to fall into a negative pattern of self-doubt, which can lead to stress and a negative outlook on life. This, in turn, can impact your health and well-being and hinder personal growth.

Living a happy life does not imply that you'll not face challenges. It means shifting your perspective of how you perceive your situation and finding solutions to overcome negative thoughts.

This book is designed to help you develop a positive mindset. Instead of feeling disempowered, you can change how you view what you're going through—and it all starts with developing a positive mindset.

Emotional and Mental Well-Being

When we face difficult situations, we often tend to amplify the problem with negative thoughts. This can lead to negative emotions like stress, anxiety, and depression. Developing a positive mindset can help you navigate through challenges and experience happiness, joy, and optimism. All of these positive emotions stem from an optimistic way of thinking.

Our thoughts have a direct impact on our emotions, and in turn, they influence our behavior.

Living a happy life does not require perfection or having everything figured out. It's about recognizing that everyone makes mistakes, and things may not always go as planned. However, we must use our experiences as opportunities to learn and grow in various aspects of our lives.

Optimism is a powerful tool that can help you develop a positive attitude toward life—even in challenging situations. It is the foundation of a happy and fulfilling life. Maintaining good mental and emotional health is crucial for your overall well-being.

Unfortunately, many people struggle with mental health issues due to various factors. Different mental health disorders can affect one's thought processes, personality, and interpersonal relationships. Therefore, taking care of your mental health is essential to lead a happy and satisfying life.

Mental health disorders can manifest in various forms, but there are common signs and symptoms that you can look out for. These include mood swings, impulsive behavior, addictions, eating disorders, disinterest in socializing, lack of motivation to set personal goals, anxiety, and depression, among other conditions. It is crucial to recognize these symptoms and seek professional help if you or someone you know is experiencing them.

Grow Your Positive Mind

I am passionate about helping people regain their power and live a well-balanced life. This book is my gift to you, which will help you cultivate a positive mindset, enhance your overall well-being, and live intentionally every day. The insights shared in each chapter of this book are based on my personal experiences and research from reputable science institutions worldwide.

Throughout the pages of this book, you will gain a comprehensive understanding of positive thinking and what it encompasses, including practices such as self-compassion, optimism, and gratitude, which can foster a positive attitude.

As you go through each chapter, you will learn the significance of identifying your strengths, addressing emotional needs, building self-esteem, and creating a healthy self-image. I've included various exercises such as mindfulness, journaling, and self-reflection to make it easier to learn and implement the concepts discussed in this book. You will also learn practical steps to set achievable goals and thrive in all aspects of your life.

Additionally, this book provides strategies to help you overcome self-doubt and resentment, heal from past experiences, and build meaningful relationships.

Remember, transformation is a process that takes consistent practice. To thrive in life, you must reprogram your mind and develop an optimistic mindset that will support your goals and future.

I hope that as you read each chapter, you'll gain valuable insight into human conditioning and enhance your well-being. This is a crucial step in identifying your mental blocks and understanding where your problems stem from. Once you identify your behavior patterns and why you behave the way you do, you can practice self-regulation.

Whether you're seeking change and personal growth, or you are a mental health specialist looking for a resource to recommend to people, this book can inspire you to live positively and with the confidence you need to accomplish your goals.

Chapter 1

TRANSFORMING YOUR LIFE: UNVEILING THE POSITIVE MINDSET

Positive anything is better than negative nothing. –Elbert Hubbard

Everyone desires to live a comfortable life, develop nurturing relationships, achieve financial independence, and lead a healthy and happy life. At the start of each year, we set our personal goals and plan how we intend to achieve them. After taking a break from work or school—we feel well-rested and ready to start the new year with optimism and excitement about what's to come.

However, as months go by, plans can fail, and unexpected events occur. You may find yourself with bills that you never budgeted for—that derail you from your financial goals. Or, your physical health suddenly takes a downturn, requiring you to take some time off from work. You may lose someone dear to you or be laid off from your job due to downsizing in the organization you work for. Life is unpredictable. A lot of things can happen that can cause you to lose the motivation you had at the beginning of the year.

The downside of all this is that when you're overwhelmed by challenges, you become susceptible to negative thinking and negative self-talk, and in this state of mind, it is not easy to maintain a positive outlook on life.

What Is a Positive Mindset?

A positive mindset can be defined as having an optimistic outlook on life—even when faced with challenging circumstances. It involves believing in yourself, having confidence in your abilities, and showing up every day—and sometimes, during days when you don't feel like getting out of bed. In other words, it is a mental and emotional attitude that focuses on the good side of life and expects positive outcomes.

Our thoughts have a significant impact on our feelings, and consequently, our feelings can influence our behaviors. Therefore, it is crucial to be mindful of your thoughts. We often think that we are always aware of our thoughts because we are thinking them, but in reality, we tend to ignore our thoughts most of the time. Our internal monologue has become so familiar that we do not pay attention to it as much as we should. However, being aware of your thoughts is important. It allows you to make informed decisions in any situation. This can be challenging at first if you have not practiced being present and paying attention to your thoughts in the past.

Observing your thoughts can help you identify and replace negative, disempowering thoughts with positive, empowering ones. Negative emotions such as fear, anxiety, sadness, anger, guilt, jealousy, and hate are a result of various factors, such as your culture, your environment, who you interact with, your diet, and your past experiences, among other factors.

By paying attention to your thought patterns, you can gain a better understanding of your perceptions.

Components of a Positive Mindset

Having a positive mindset means having a state of mind that is shaped by empowering thoughts. According to a study published on the Nature Communications website in 2020, the average person has around 6,000 thoughts per day (Tseng and Poppenk, 2020). This emphasizes the significance of being mindful of the thoughts we entertain, as they can greatly influence our overall outlook on life. However, it is important to note that this does not mean disregarding negative thoughts that may arise from time to time. When cultivating a positive mindset, be mindful not to get trapped in toxic positivity. While having a positive mindset is considered a healthy state of mind, extreme positivity can be harmful.

Toxic positivity is when you avoid negative experiences and emotions by pretending to be happy and positive when faced with adversity. It can be harmful because you put a lot of pressure on yourself to appear cheerful in difficult situations.

Even though it is often experienced with good intentions, if left unchecked, toxic positivity can lead to feeling overwhelmed by the very emotions you are trying to avoid.

If you ever find yourself concealing your emotions and pretending that everything is okay when, in reality, you feel overwhelmed, remember that it is completely okay to confide in someone you trust. Do not feel ashamed to express how you feel. Instead, allow yourself to feel your emotions—no matter how uncomfortable they may be.

Revealing the things that hurt and make you feel powerless is not a sign of weakness. It simply shows that you care about your well-being enough to speak up and seek the help you require.

What Makes up a Positive Mindset?

Now that we've defined what a positive mindset is let us delve into the factors that can foster a positive mindset. One way to better understand the components of a positive mindset is to think of your thoughts based on time frames.

Your state of mind is influenced by different factors. These include your perception of the past and present circumstances, as well as the future.

To gain an understanding of how your thoughts affect you, you can categorize them into:

- **Past positive thoughts**: This involves viewing past experiences positively. For example, reminiscing about fun times with childhood friends.

- **Current positive thoughts**: This involves seeing your present circumstances in a positive light and choosing to focus more on the good that surrounds you even in difficult situations.

- **Positive thoughts about the future**: This requires you to have positive expectations about the future and expect positive outcomes.

- **Positive self-focused thoughts**: This involves having a healthy self-image, self-love, and self-confidence. It means focusing more on your positive attributes.

- **Other-focused positive thoughts**: These are thoughts that are mostly focused on others, such as empathy, kindness, and trust.

By categorizing your thoughts in this manner, you can gain a better understanding of your emotions and take control of them.

The Benefits of a Positive Mindset

Maintaining a positive mindset is the basis of a happier and healthier life. It helps you to live your life with a light-hearted approach and appreciate even the smallest things, such as a kind gesture from a stranger, the sound of birds chirping outside, the sun setting on the horizon on a late summer afternoon, or the fact that you have access to clean water.

Developing a positive mindset can help you see the good that already exists. Focusing more on your blessings rather than on the challenging aspects of your life makes it easier to be grateful. Not only does optimism create positive attitudes and emotions, but it can also lower the chances of health conditions such as high blood pressure, heart disease, chronic pain caused by stress, and depression (Mayo Clinic Staff, n.d.).

Optimism can boost your confidence and enable you to take on new challenges that you probably would not have taken in the past. It pushes you out of your comfort zone to do what is necessary to achieve your goals and essentially transform your life.

If you seek positive change in your life but are unsure how positive thinking can help you achieve this, here are some of the benefits of developing a positive mindset that can inspire you to start reframing your thoughts.

The Physical Benefits of a Positive Mindset

A positive mindset involves looking and expecting to find solutions to challenges. When you are faced with adversity, you do not ignore your circumstances, nor do you allow challenges to disempower you. Instead, you find ways to overcome them. You understand that it is your responsibility to steer your life in the direction you want it to go.

Below are some of the health benefits of developing a positive mindset.

- **It can increase your life span:** Research carried out at the National Academy of Sciences shows that optimistic people live longer and have higher chances of living past the age of 85 (Topor, 2019). The results of the study were based on the responses participants gave on their views on several statements on positive thinking. The Optimism-Pessimism scale (Malinchoc et al. 1995) was used to measure the personality of each participant, and both men and women who had a positive outlook had a longer life span, living up to age 85. This highlights the impact optimism has on your physical well-being.

- **It improves your immune system and makes you resilient to diseases:** Recent studies have provided ample evidence that our minds play a key role in improving our immune system and making us more resilient to diseases like the common cold, diabetes, and cancer (Shankar et al. 2020). Therefore, developing a positive mindset can increase your ability to fight off illnesses and maintain better health.

- **It lowers the chances of suffering a heart attack:** A positive mindset can lower your chances of suffering chronic diseases, such as cardiovascular disease and other infections, by improving your immune system.

- **It reduces blood pressure:** Optimism can reduce stress, lowering blood pressure and leading to a healthier heart (Tello, 2019). Positive thinking, practicing gratitude, and living joyfully increase your levels of serotonin—the happy hormone and can reduce heart rate and blood pressure during stressful times.

- **It is an effective stress-management technique:** The results of a study conducted on patients with kidney problems in 2021 show that positive thinking significantly reduced stress and anxiety in the study group in comparison to the control group (Shokrpour et al. 2021). By remaining optimistic in adverse times, you can lower your stress levels and achieve a calm state of mind that allows you to think rationally and come up with solutions to resolve challenges.

- **It increases your ability to endure:** Dealing with challenges can be overwhelming, but keeping a positive mindset can provide the necessary strength and ideas to overcome obstacles. A positive outlook helps you concentrate on finding solutions and the resources you need to solve a crisis, which in turn improves your problem-solving skills.

- **It improves your physical well-being:** Positive thinking not only enhances your ability to cope in stressful situations, but it also improves your physical well-being. When you feel optimistic, your brain produces endorphins—the feel-good hormones like dopamine and serotonin that can reduce stress and improve your mood.

While optimism is heritable and can be linked to our genes, science proves that our environment and the information we're exposed to have a significant impact on how we see the world (Solan, 2021). Therefore, it is crucial to be mindful of the components that foster a positive mindset, as we have discussed above, and observe your environment when you feel out of balance.

The Mental Benefits of a Positive Mindset

When you are going through a difficult period, it seems almost impossible to maintain a positive attitude because, at the back of your mind, you know that you are facing a crisis. However, developing a positive mindset can open up new ways for you to tackle challenges and improve your problem-solving skills. It fosters mental and emotional wellness. This usually happens because a positive mind focuses more on your strengths, finding solutions, and expressing deep gratitude. This state of being heightens your awareness, improves emotional regulation, and empowers you to live purposefully, build strong social connections, and succeed in life.

Developing a positive mindset can:

- **Boost your creativity:** Do you remember, growing up—how you used to role-play with your friends? Life seemed easy back then. You would let your mind take you to places that your physical body could not. You dreamed big and believed you could be, do, and have whatever you desired. More importantly, you did not let minor setbacks stop you from learning. As we grow, we lose the curiosity we had when we were younger that enabled us to learn. We allow our circumstances to dictate whether or not we lead happy lives. Positive thinking and creativity are closely linked. A positive mindset can boost your creativity and generate constructive ideas and solutions.

- **Improve your problem-solving skills:** Maintaining a positive attitude amid a crisis can help you stay composed. Rather than focus on the problem, you focus on finding the right solution. For example, at work, you may find yourself in a disagreement with a coworker over a work-related issue. Instead of pointing fingers at each other, a positive mind allows you to remain calm and look for a practical way to resolve the issue. If it is above your abilities, you will seek help from someone more knowledgeable in that field.

- **Clear your mind and promote rational thinking:** Often, when our minds perceive a possible threat to our well-being, our first reaction is the fight or flight response. This is a result of associating an event or object with past negative experiences. For example, say you had a bad experience in the past while giving an important presentation at work. You may have lost confidence and messed up the entire presentation. Chances are, when you find yourself having to give a presentation, you may experience psychological fear, which triggers your current reaction (Sutton, 2022). When faced with a perceived threat, our bodies release hormones that prepare us to either face the situation or run to seek safety. Maintaining a positive mindset enables you to slow down and think rationally.

- **Boost your mood:** When you are stressed, your brain releases endorphins (chemicals that help relieve stress and pain). This can significantly boost your mood. Taking on physical activity such as working out, walking, biking, or hiking can also increase endorphins in your body and make you feel better. So, when you feel overwhelmed, take a walk-in nature, and you will be amazed at how grounded you will feel.

- **Improve your coping skills:** Optimism enables you to look for effective ways to deal with challenges. This allows you to process your emotions, practice self-care, and overcome negative self-talk.

- **Reduce stress and depression:** Optimism can reduce stress levels and lower the risk of depression. When you maintain a positive outlook even in the face of adversity, you build the confidence you need to keep moving forward and believe that everything will eventually work out. This allows you to stay on course and keep working on achieving your goals.

At its core, a positive mindset is the key to living a fulfilled life.

Characteristics of a Positive Mindset

Like any other personality trait, there are common signs of having a positive mindset. These include:

- **Optimism**: That is, maintaining a positive outlook even when your back is pressed against the wall.

- **Gratitude**: Being thankful for the blessings you already have, such as your loved ones, a kind gesture from a stranger, your job, or appreciating simple things like the sounds of nature, for example, ocean waves or a stream passing over rocks.

- **Acceptance** : That is, embracing who you are and not allowing your circumstances to disempower you. It involves enduring a crisis but knowing that nothing lasts forever and that whatever situation you may be in will pass.

- **Resilience**: This is the ability to build the strength you need to gracefully go through difficult times.

- **Integrity**: Being kind and avoiding talking negatively to others and yourself.

How to Develop a Positive Mindset

We have learned about the benefits of developing a positive mindset and its significance in leading a happier and healthier life.

Maintaining a positive attitude toward life involves living with a light-hearted approach and appreciating even the smallest things that life offers. It allows you to focus more on the positive side of life rather than on the challenging aspects— which fosters gratitude.

Now that you have an idea of what a positive mindset is and how it can benefit you, let us delve into how you can develop it and reframe your thoughts.

Spend Time Developing a Positive Mindset

Learning a new skill takes time and practice to master. The same applies to developing a positive mindset and reframing your thinking processes. Positive changes in your thinking patterns may not be visible immediately, but with time, the tiny things you do each day can have a significant impact on your outlook.

To develop a positive mindset, be intentional and set aside time each day to practice positive thinking. It could be 5 minutes or 30 minutes each day, depending on your lifestyle. It does not matter how much time you put into the practice; what matters is that you implement these techniques consistently to achieve effective results.

Practice Gratitude

Practicing gratitude can have a significant impact on your life, making it more fulfilling. Studies show that gratitude has a host of physical and mental benefits, which include improved mood, immunity, and sleep (Logan, 2022). Maintaining an attitude of gratitude can be effective in reducing stress, anxiety, depression, and the risk of other illnesses.

If you are feeling out of balance, try starting your day by thinking about something or someone you are grateful for. You may be grateful for having a family that adores and appreciates you or the kind gesture the lady at your local bakery extends to you each time you go shopping. You do not need to experience something huge to practice gratitude. Even the smallest things we experience daily can have a significant impact on our lives. For example, when a stranger compliment you, this alone can uplift your mood if you are feeling downcast.

Take sometime during the day to text, call, or leave a note for the people you are grateful for. You will be amazed at how it will improve your relationships and strengthen your connections.

It is much easier to be thankful when we acknowledge our blessings than when we focus on everything that is going wrong in our lives. When you appreciate what you have, you open yourself up to more joy and positivity.

Taking time to reflect on all the things you are thankful for each day can have a positive impact on your self-esteem and self-confidence. It can help you develop a healthier self-image. So, why not take a moment today to think about the things that you appreciate? Write them down in your journal and observe how this can significantly change your mood!

Think of Positive Ideas

To make it easier to practice positive thinking, make it a habit to retrieve positive information from your brain. I know that it may not be easy to remain optimistic all the time, especially when you are going through a difficult period in your life;

however, constantly focusing on positive thoughts can make the process easier with time.

One way you can start reframing your thoughts is by writing down positive affirmations or posting notes around the house. You could write your affirmations on a Post-it note and stick them on your bathroom mirror or your workstation.

Your positive affirmation could look something like:

- "Today is going to be a great day."

- "I have the power to transform my life."

- "I am worthy of love."

Repeat positive statements to yourself every day, in the morning and the evening. By doing so, you train your brain to receive more positive information.

Focus On Your Strengths

Low self-esteem and self-worth often result in self-doubt and negative self-talk. It can make you focus more on your negative traits, mistakes, and failures rather than focusing on your positive qualities, the things you do best, and your accomplishments.

Despite all your weaknesses, you also have strengths—these include the skills you have acquired from personal experience, your natural gifts, and your talents. Focusing more on your strengths will probably serve you better than focusing on your weaknesses. It can make you feel positive about yourself and help you develop a positive self-image.

Focus On Your Positive Attributes

Everyone has a good side and a bad side. But we often let the bad side override the good side. However, the world can benefit more if we choose to express the good side rather than allowing negativity to dictate how we live our lives. When you see yourself in a positive light, you get to know yourself better. This paves the way for you to discover the good side of your personality and positive attributes such as kindness, empathy, compassion, politeness, peacefulness, and patience, to name a few.

Whether you believe it or not, you have positive qualities, and if you have not discovered them yet, make a list of your strengths and the things you are good at and refer to them from time to time. This will program your brain to focus on your strengths rather than your weaknesses.

Practice Self-Compassion

We often allow the inner critic to sit in the driver's seat and steer our lives. When we make mistakes or fail at what we attempt to do, we tend to be harsh on ourselves and forget the times we did something right or accomplished something significant.

Self-compassion is key to developing a positive mindset. Be kind and gentle with yourself as you would be to a small child. Celebrate your wins every chance you get, and when your plans fail, or things do not work out as you had hoped they would, remember that failure is an opportunity to learn. Cultivate a positive attitude and believe that when you make a second or third attempt, you will be better at what you do than you were before.

21

Practice Self-Care

Self-care and self-love go hand in hand. Love yourself enough to take care of your well-being. Your entire life hinges upon how well you take care of all areas of your life—that is, your physical, mental, emotional, spiritual, and financial wellness, as well as your relationships. Practicing self-care can help you experience more positivity in your life and create memorable experiences.

When you are healthy and grounded, you can build healthier relationships, become mindful of the information you expose yourself to, and create beliefs that serve you.

We have learned what a positive mindset is and how you can cultivate optimism. Perhaps you are unsure of where to start your journey. Maybe for the longest time, you have believed or heard people say that you are not good enough, educated enough, or you do not have the required skills for a particular assignment. And for this reason, self-doubt always cripples you and gets in the way of your success—leaving you frustrated.

When you develop a positive mindset, you can learn ways to identify your strengths and how to embrace them so you can unleash your full potential.

Chapter 2

EMBRACING YOUR STRENGTHS: UNLEASHING YOUR FULL POTENTIAL

Be yourself, everyone else is already taken.
–Oscar Wilde

Accomplishing anything worthwhile in life requires believing in yourself and in your abilities. Unfortunately, most people tend to focus more on fixing their weaknesses to succeed in life and not pay much attention to improving on what they already do best.

While it is not a bad idea to fix your weaknesses to get better results, identifying your strengths and nurturing your natural gifts can increase your chances of success in your career and relationships.

In an article published by CNBC in 2019, Dr. Marcus Burckingham shared the results of a study on how to win at work. The study shows that employees participate and utilize their abilities when they engage in effective and empowering work activities (Stevens and Castillo, 2019).

In the article, Dr. Burckingham suggests that employees should participate in activities that give them fulfillment and strengthen their intellect. This is because, often, these are the activities that people excel in. He further explains that when we use our strengths to carry out an activity, it usually comes naturally to us and increases our chances of succeeding.

This phenomenon not only applies to your career but to all areas of your life. If you want to excel and thrive in your relationships, spiritual life, finances, and overall well-being, you should determine your natural tendencies and skills and focus on nurturing them.

The Importance of Developing Your Strengths

The foundation of personal development involves adopting concepts and ideas that encourage growth. When we are pessimistic and negatively view ourselves, we get in the way of our growth. Sometimes, it is not that we do not have the necessary skills to succeed in what we do but that we tend to talk ourselves out of taking the first step because of fear.

Most of us are afraid of failure, while some fear judgment. And sometimes, we let the fear of the unknown keep us in one place and stunt our growth. Instead of pushing ourselves out of our comfort zone, we often prefer to remain in the same familiar place than attempt something new. But the thing is, we are not meant to stay in one place. Our souls yearn for growth, which is why we experience periods of dissatisfaction at some point in our lives and a need to do and be more than what we have become.

Each one of us has a purpose to fulfill on earth. You were born with natural gifts and talents that can help you accomplish your purpose. Whether or not you have a college degree, there are things you are good at that come naturally to you. It could be your ability to communicate in a way that makes people listen, leadership, arts and crafts, singing, running, listening, teaching, or peacemaking. There are some of the abilities you may have that come naturally to you that you can use to make the world a better place.

As we grow, we learn different skills that enable us to carry out certain tasks and complete assignments. These skills include technical expertise and knowledge-based skills such as learning different languages, reading, and writing, among others. Through constant practice, we learn ways to perfect these skills, and they end up becoming a part of who we are.

Why Focus on Your Strengths?

Focusing on your strong attributes is important to your success in life because:

- **It makes achieving your desired results much easier:** When you do the things that you are good at and enjoy doing, you increase your efficiency and chances of achieving your desired results.

- **It can improve your mood:** Focusing on your strengths is a mood booster. It promotes a healthy state of mind and lowers levels of stress and depression (McQuaid, 2014).

- **It can enhance life satisfaction:** If you want to feel happier and more satisfied with your life, focus more on your strengths and less on your weaknesses. For example, your character strengths. These include creativity, passion for learning, judgment, honesty, kindness, humility, humor, self-regulation, and spirituality (Berns-Zare, 2019). Character strengths express who you are and support your thinking, how you feel, and participation. Focusing more on these strengths can help you build empathy, develop understanding, and achieve professional and personal goals.

- **It can boost your self-confidence:** Studies show that developing your strengths has a positive impact on your productivity, self-confidence, goal-oriented thinking, interpersonal relationships, and career and academic success (Hodges, 2005).

- **It promotes growth and development:** When you use your talents coupled with the knowledge and skills you have, you start building your strengths and increase your chances of success.

- **It improves your creativity and effectiveness:** Research shows that building our strengths promotes feelings of authenticity, concentration, and liveliness that can help us adapt quickly to change, be more creative, develop proactive behaviors, and pay attention to detail (Forest and Dubreuil, 2014).

There is so much you can learn about yourself and your abilities when you devote time to develop your positive attributes. When you identify and use your strengths, you reignite your curiosity, connect with your creative side, build self-confidence, and begin to feel optimistic.

How to Identify Your Strengths

Whether or not you believe that you are capable of achieving greatness, remember that you have gifts and talents that you have not fully utilized yet—that need nurturing and can be beneficial to you. You also have skills that you have acquired over the years that you can use to create a better life for yourself. Here are a few ideas on how you can begin to identify your strengths.

Change Self-Perception Using the SWOT Analysis

Changing your self-perception is a process. It takes time and commitment to reprogram your mind and reframe your thinking processes. Imagine how long it took you to develop your belief system. It did not happen overnight. It took years of learning and going through different experiences to build the beliefs that have shaped your life.

Changing how you see and feel about yourself is the same. It is a process of unlearning your old beliefs, letting go of behaviors that no longer serve you, adopting a new way of thinking, and developing habits that support your growth. It requires putting in place a strategy that will help you reframe your perceptions. One way you can do this is by using the SWOT Analysis.

The SWOT Analysis is a technique used by organizations and individuals to identify strengths, weaknesses, opportunities, and threats to their success. This technique takes into consideration the internal and external factors that affect your success. It uncovers the opportunities you would not usually recognize.

27

If you view yourself using the SWOT Analysis, you can separate yourself from others and develop the natural gifts and specialized talents you need to thrive in your personal and professional life.

How to Perform a Personal SWOT Analysis

In your journal, make a list of your strengths, weaknesses, opportunities, and threats:

Strengths

- The advantages you have that other people don't. These may include skills, education, qualifications, and personal connections.

- The things you do better than others.

- The resources you have at your disposal.

- The things others see as your strongest attributes.

- Personal values that are not displayed by others.

- The achievements you are most proud of.

- Your social connections that no one else is a part of.

- Influential people you are connected to.

When listing your strengths, think of them in comparison to other people, but take your perspective into account as well. For example, a compliment from your boss for your excellent negotiation skills and the ability to close sales compared to your colleagues.

If you have difficulty identifying your strengths, make a list of your positive characteristics, such as:

- honesty

- kindness

- integrity

- humility

- Courage

- perseverance

Next, make a list of your weaknesses.

Weaknesses

These include:

- the things you avoid doing because of a lack of confidence.

- the things people around you deem as weaknesses.

- your negative habits. For example, if you lack organization skills, are always late, or have difficulties managing stress.

- personality traits that hinder your personal growth. For example, fear can prevent you from making contributions at work that would be of value to your organization.

Think of your weaknesses from an internal and external point of view. Also, consider if the people around you see weaknesses in you that you do not see. Be objective and honest when writing your list. This way, you can face your truth and work on improving the areas you need to work on.

After identifying your weaknesses, make a list of the opportunities available to you.

Opportunities

These include:

- the resources available to you, such as technology and the people you meet on online platforms.

- the growth levels in your industry. Identify how you can utilize the demand in the current market.

- your advisors, and the people who can help you.

- movements at work or school that you can be a part of and how you can contribute to.

- the things that others fail to do that you can take advantage of.

- a gap or need to be filled in your community, religious setting, workplace, or school.

- customer complaints (if you are employed). Could you come up with a solution to customer needs?

- networking events, conferences, or taking a study course.

- taking on a project that offers an opportunity to learn new skills like leadership.

When making a list of opportunities available to you, consider your strengths and see if you can unlock opportunities by using them. Then, look at your weaknesses to see if eliminating them can unlock new possibilities.

Next, identify the threats to your success.

Threats

These include:

- the obstacles you are facing at work, school, financially, or in your relationships.

- your competitors in business, work, or in school.

- changes in the demand for what you specialize in.

- advancements in technology and the possibility of being replaced at work.

- weaknesses that pose a threat to your overall success, such as defensiveness and failure to process negative criticism.

When working on achieving your goals, take stock of where you are and acknowledge the things you can do rather than focus on your limitations. Develop a growth mindset and recognize that to succeed in life, you must always strive for improvement.

Acknowledge What You Are Good At

We have grown accustomed to focusing more on the things we cannot do and trying to fix them rather than focusing on what we do best. Often, the things we are good at come naturally to us, and they have become second nature, such that we do not recognize them as strengths. For some reason, it is easier to spot your mistakes than to celebrate your wins, no matter how small they are.

Developing your strengths involves recognizing what you are good at and cultivating your strongest attributes. It is about accepting and acknowledging your abilities and taking steps to improve every day. If, for instance, you play the piano, seek opportunities to improve your skills. Focus on playing the piano instead of playing other musical instruments you are not good at. Improving on your strengths can help you build self-confidence while perfecting your skills.

Use the 80% Rule

Spending more time focusing on your weaknesses is not an effective way for personal growth. We often do not find pleasure in doing tasks that we are not good at. At some point, we stop trying, but when you cultivate your strengths, nothing can stop you. The thought of being good at what you do fuels you to keep going even when the odds are against you.

When learning to identify your strengths, spend 80% of your time developing your strengths.

To help you with this exercise, ask yourself the following questions:

- How can you utilize your skills and improve them?

- Who can you spend time with who is an expert in your field?

- What resources do you need to help you develop your skills?

Change is not easy. When you are accustomed to a certain way of thinking, adopting new habits and changing your outlook can be challenging at first. But just like learning any other skill, you become better at it with practice.

If, perhaps, you are an events planner and you have only been planning small events for your organization, look for an opportunity to plan a big event—it could be in your community or local church. Knock down the walls of self-doubt and believe that you can do it. You will be amazed at how proud you will be of yourself when you accomplish something significant.

You have what it takes to achieve your goals. What you need is to tap into the unlimited power that is within you and use your natural gifts and talents to create the life you envision. And it all starts with self-reflection and developing a positive outlook on life.

Chapter 3:

THE POWER WITHIN: DISCOVERING POSITIVITY THROUGH SELF-REFLECTION

You can, you should, and if you're brave enough to start, you will. –Stephen King

When faced with a challenge, do you look at the brighter side of things, or does your mind start racing, and you think of all the things that could go wrong and how bad the situation can get?

When thinking about your life, do you see the glass as half full or half empty? As much as we wish to remain optimistic in any situation, there are times when it feels impossible. When we are pressed by challenges, it becomes easier to perceive negative outcomes than to focus on the possibilities of achieving positive results. It takes great effort to remain optimistic amid a crisis.

We all face difficult times at some point in our lives, but we also have the power to focus on the positive side and have hope that things will work out. Optimism enables you to see more of the good events that happen in your life than bad ones. It allows you to develop coping skills that can help you navigate your way through challenges.

Developing a positive mindset requires taking some time to practice self-reflection. Cultivating self-awareness, understanding your identity, and identifying your unique qualities involves doing some introspection from time to time. This can help you align with your values, and it promotes emotional stability and self-regulation.

Building a healthy state of mind requires accepting all parts of you, both positive and negative, and integrating them into your identity. Just because you are cultivating a positive mindset does not mean you must ignore your negative traits. These could be negative thinking and negative self-talk, pessimism, fear, or apathy. What it means is you invest your time to figure out your unique qualities and how you can utilize them.

Identifying Your Good Qualities

There are numerous positive character traits one can have. Learning to identify them can help you take advantage of them in your personal growth.

Here are a few positive traits to look out for.

- **Agreeableness:** This means that you are cooperative, kind, friendly, and polite. It also means that you exhibit prosocial behavior.

- **Conscientiousness:** This means you are well-organized, thorough, and goal-oriented, and you can adhere to rules.

- **Extroversion:** This means that you are sociable and confident in social situations

- **Non-discriminatory:** This means you treat everyone fairly and equally—regardless of their gender, race, religion, or physical and characteristic differences.

- **Openness:** This means that you are receptive and accessible. It also means you are willing to learn new ideas.

Other positive qualities you can identify in you include the following:

Positive Interpersonal Traits

- **A great leader:** This means you can guide and enable others to work together to accomplish a goal they would not accomplish individually. A good leader inspires innovation in people to achieve something great.

- **Compassionate:** This means you are warm-hearted, understanding, and caring toward others.

- **Empathetic:** This refers to your ability to understand and share other people's feelings.

- **Generous:** This is your ability to offer others help. This means that you have a noble spirit, and you can extend kindness and sometimes financial aid to those who need it.

- **Humble :** This means you are modest, submissive, and respectful.

- **Supportive:** This refers to your ability to encourage and reassure others. It also means you are caring and understanding.

- **Spontaneous:** This means that you act out the natural feelings that arise from momentary impulses and come from within you without planning or being forced.

Positive Intellectual Traits

- **Analytical:** This means you are inquisitive and like to examine things in detail.

- **Intelligent:** This means you are smart, and you have a high degree of mental capacity. It also means that your mind is sharp, you think rationally, and have good judgment (*Thesaurus Results for Intelligent,* n.d.)

- **Observant:** This means that you pay close attention to things and people.

- **Decisive:** This refers to your ability to make decisions quickly, without any doubts.

- **Curious:** This means you are eager to learn new ideas.

- **Innovative:** This is your ability to come up with new ideas and concepts and use them to create products and services.

How to Develop
Positive Personality Traits

By now, you have an idea of what a positive mindset looks like and why identifying and utilizing your strengths is important to your overall success. While you may focus more on the negative aspects of your personality, the good news is your personality is not carved in stone. Through practice and persistence, you can develop your positive traits.

Now, let us dive deep and learn how you can start developing your positive personality traits.

Identify Your Negative Characteristic Traits

We have discussed a lot about positive traits; now, let us look at your negative traits as part of the process of developing positive ones. While you may have a positive side, you also have a negative side, and to learn to cultivate your positive side or strengths, you must identify your negative, disempowering tendencies and understand how they affect your personal growth. For example, if you have a fear of public speaking, this could get in the way of you sharing your ideas and concepts that could be useful to others.

Choose One Trait You Would Like to Change

Once you have listed your negative traits, pick one that you would like to improve. Start with smaller traits that can add to bigger ones. For example, if you want to improve your agreeableness, you can start by being kind and easygoing.

39

Adopt Positive Behaviors and Practices

The most efficient way to improve negative personality traits is to practice the opposite. This can be difficult at first, but applying these concepts will become much easier with time.

For example, if you are an impatient person, one way you can start to improve and learn to be patient is by taking a step back and doing breathwork. When you notice signs that your impatient side is taking control, take a deep breath in and slowly breathe out. Repeat this 10 times—until you feel calm.

Other calming exercises like mindfulness, meditation, and journaling can help you during the process and remind you to relax and be present.

Seek Mentorship

The journey of transformation can be challenging, and sometimes, you may need someone to hold your hand. Ask someone you trust who has the characteristics you want to improve for advice and support. It could be a therapist or a loved one. They may teach you and hold you accountable for achieving your goals. For example, if you have a quick temper, joining an anger management program and pairing with someone who has overcome anger issues can be helpful.

Be Persistent

Developing a new way of thinking does not happen overnight. It takes time and persistence to achieve your goal. Try not to seek perfection but embrace your mistakes and learn from them. For example, if you lose your temper when someone triggers you, despite your efforts to be more patient. Accept your faults while you work on emotional regulation, and bear in mind that the benefits of developing a positive mindset and self-awareness far exceed the pain and discomfort you may feel throughout the process. Therefore, keep the end goal in mind. It will fuel your desire for transformation.

Steps to Transform Your Self-Image

Do you have a healthy sense of self? Or do you criticize and judge yourself for your mistakes and flaws? Your self-image is how you view yourself at a conscious and unconscious level. It is an emotional conclusion you make about your worth.

We develop a self-image through interacting with others and interpreting their reactions toward us and what they think of us. While someone else's opinion of you may be distorted by a lot of factors, such as their worldview and societal norms, we often believe these opinions to be true and, therefore, create an inaccurate reflection of ourselves.

This leads us to compare ourselves to others. We compare ourselves against what our families and society expect from us, for example, achieving career success or being a good parent. These expectations affect how we perceive ourselves.

To develop a healthy self-image, get to know yourself and not create an image based on other people's opinions. This involves assessing your appearance, personal values, thoughts, and behaviors as an individual and compared to others.

Now, why is developing your self-image important? It is because a healthy self-image is the key to self-acceptance and building self-confidence.

The following are the other benefits of developing a positive self-image:

- You act confidently—without guilt.

- You can handle constructive criticism.

- You see everyone as your equal.

- You seek out positive people like yourself.

- You do not allow yourself to be manipulated by others.

- You recognize your positive and negative feelings, and you are not afraid to share them with others.

- You try out different things that lead to sustainability and a balanced life.

- You view challenges as opportunities to learn and grow.

- You have a high sense of self-value.

- You do not dwell on the past.

- You value other people.

To start developing your self-image, here are a few practices you can do that will help you change the way you see yourself.

Do a Self-Image Assessment

A negative self-image often leads to feelings of inadequacy and results in depression. However, developing a healthy self-image, on the other hand, can help you take criticism and face challenges without judgment. It enables you to take a step back when you face a situation beyond your control, with an understanding that you are not your circumstances, failures, and weaknesses. It also allows you to accept your outcomes and learn from your experiences.

To carry out a self-assessment test, ask yourself the following questions:

- **What do you love most about yourself?** If you have never taken the time to sit and reflect on what you love most about yourself, try it. You'll be surprised at how good you feel about yourself. In your journal, make a list of the things you love about yourself. Think deeply, and not only write your physical aspects, such as a nice smile, but also include things like your emotional stability, ability to help others, wisdom, and discernment.

- **Would you say the same words you say to yourself to your best friend?** The words you speak to yourself every day have an impact on your thoughts, feelings, and behavior. Now, you would never say to a friend, "'You're so dumb," or "You're stupid," would you? Instead, you would speak kindly to them when they make a mistake and reassure them that everything will be okay. Treat yourself as you would a friend. Speak positive words to yourself daily and watch your self-esteem improve.

- **Do you show yourself that you are worthy?** People with a low sense of self-worth often feel they do not deserve to spoil themselves. They often prioritize other people's needs and ignore theirs. But buying yourself something beautiful that you've always wanted or taking a class to upgrade your skills can significantly improve your sense of self-worth. Meeting your needs is part of self-care and is beneficial to your well-being.

- **Do you have healthy boundaries in place?** Without boundaries, you become susceptible to being pushed around. Setting healthy boundaries can teach you to say "No" to people who want to take advantage of you.

Make a List of All Your Good Traits

Most of us allow the harsh inner critic to control us and point out our mistakes. We pay less attention to our good qualities, and this often leads to a negative view of ourselves and a pessimistic outlook on life. It is difficult to have a positive outlook when you do not have a healthy relationship with yourself.

Living a happier life starts with changing the way you see yourself, and you can start by loving every bit of yourself and acknowledging your good traits while you work on improving your imperfections.

If you struggle with low self-esteem, it may be difficult to identify your good qualities, but not impossible. Here are a few exercises you can do to discover your good qualities:

- **Applaud yourself for your acts of kindness no matter how small they are:** For example, helping an elderly person at the grocery store, complimenting a colleague, or offering to help a friend when they are in need.

- **Practice positive self-talk:** Self-value is essential to building a healthy self-image. While self-worth is your sense of worth, self-value goes beyond knowing your worth. It involves your actions toward what you value most rather than your feelings about yourself compared to other people. When you value yourself, your actions align with those values, and when you make mistakes, you understand that you are not perfect and take mistakes as a learning curve. Instead of being too hard on yourself, you speak gently and lovingly to yourself.

- **Practice positive affirmations** : I know some people find it awkward to speak to themselves, but building any relationship requires communication. It is the same with building a relationship with yourself. Try speaking positively to yourself. Changing a negative perspective of yourself starts with learning to speak positively to and about yourself. To help you with this exercise, identify an area you need to work on and write down positive affirmations concerning that area in your journal. For example, if you struggle with your self-image, you can write, "I am at peace in my body, mind, and spirit" or "I am worthy." The more you practice positive affirmations, the more they will be embedded in your mind.

Get Your Loved Ones to List Your Positive Characteristics

Sometimes, it's best to ask the people in your life to give you an honest view of your strengths. They will give you an unbiased opinion that can help you identify your positive traits, some of which you may not be aware of. By doing this, you'd be surprised at the number of things you are more than capable of doing.

45

Set Attainable and Quantifiable Goals for Yourself

A goal is something you want to achieve that is aligned with your values and personal vision. In other words, it is a dream with a timeline.

There are different types of goals you can set for yourself. These can be categorized as:

- **Personal goals:** These are goals related to your health, relationships, and recreational activities.

- **Professional goals:** These are your career goals, such as promotions, skills development, and job performance.

- **Financial goals:** These are goals for personal finances, for example, budgeting, saving for a car, investing for retirement, and paying off debt.

- **Academic goals:** These are goals for upgrading your education, such as getting a degree and learning a new skill.

- **Social goals:** These are goals related to your social life, such as networking, attending social gatherings, improving communication, and making friends.

To set goals that are easy to accomplish, you must identify your long-term, bigger goals and break them down into short-term, smaller, achievable goals. For example, you can break down your yearly goals into monthly goals, weekly goals, and daily goals.

For a goal to qualify as a long-term goal, you must consider how long it will take you to achieve it. Long-term goals usually take several months to years to accomplish, and short-term goals normally take a few weeks, days, or months.

The Importance of Setting Goals

Setting goals has numerous benefits for your growth and development. It gives you a road map to follow to achieve your desired results and the steps you need to take to turn your dreams into reality. For example, say your five-year goal is to purchase a new home. To achieve it, you may set short-term monthly goals to pay off your debt in the first year, create an extra stream of income, and save for a down payment for your new home.

Setting long-term goals and acting upon them is an effective way to turn your dreams into reality. It provides a clear picture of where you are headed in life and the motivation you need to achieve your goals.

Not only does goal setting give you direction, but it also gives you control over your life. You do not leave things to chance but take the initiative to accomplish your dreams.

How to Set Achievable Goals

The following steps can help you get started with goal setting:

- **Consider the things that inspire you:** Goal setting involves identifying your passions, values, and the things that inspire you. Your goals must be important to you and give you a sense of pride when you accomplish them.

- **Set goals you have control over:** If you set goals that are out of your control or depend on other people, chances are you won't have the power to control your outcomes. When setting goals, consider your abilities and what you can control.

- **Visualize the future:** Take some time to think about what you want your future to look like in detail. If your goal is to apply for a promotion at work, consider taking a course and learning a new skill. It could be a sales and marketing course, project management, or business administration. If you want to improve your finances, consider how much you want to earn monthly, weekly, or daily. What skills do you have that you can monetize? Do you want to be employed or work as an independent contractor? And how many hours are you prepared to commit each day or each week to meet your goal? Asking yourself these questions will give you a clear picture of the steps you need to take to achieve your goals.

Confront Your Biases in Thinking

A bias is a preference toward an idea, group, or concept that influences our decisions (Gould, 2023). Society, cultures, and our personal experiences shape our beliefs, and we act upon them either consciously or unconsciously.

The judgmental beliefs we hold can lead to discriminatory behaviors. They can affect the way we interact with others and influence our thoughts, attitudes, and behaviors toward others. For example, gender bias leads to discriminatory attitudes toward people based on their gender and treating them differently. This affects the ability to socialize in healthy ways and can result in unfair treatment of others and unequal opportunities.

Biases can lead to misinterpretation of events in our lives and how we perceive people. One way to overcome biases is to challenge them and understand that our ideas are nothing more than concepts. They do not define who we are as people.

When you understand that people are more than the labels we place on them, but that they have skills, abilities, and qualities just like you, you start seeing everyone as equal to you, and your view and interpretation of your experiences change as well.

Recognize and Investigate the Effects of Labels from Your Childhood

Some of the difficulties we face emotionally as adults stem from labels that were placed on us in childhood.

Labels used to categorize children can be medical, such as attention deficit hyperactivity disorder (ADHD), or social, emotional, and behavioral challenges. These labels are often used in educational systems to place children in categories based on their learning abilities, behavior, and educational needs.

The use of labels can be detrimental to a child's growth and development. Being treated differently often leads to marginalization and bullying in schools and societies.

As children grow, they change, but the labels remain embedded in them. Often, people carry the labels and the negative reputations associated with them from childhood into adulthood.

Social, emotional, and behavioral labels often identify the problem within a person—individualizing the issue but failing to address the underlying cause. This makes it difficult to overcome these labels through a holistic approach (Plows, 2014).

Labels focus on the difficult aspects of a person and overlook their strengths and abilities. By confronting and evaluating labels placed on us from childhood, we can gain an understanding that not all of them are negative. Labels can be an effective way to meet people with similar experiences and encourage a positive group identity where you can receive support.

Avoid Comparing Yourself to Other People

With the increase of social media platforms and new trends that come up every day, it can be difficult not to compare yourself to others. You may feel that you are not enough because you do not have a body like a Vogue magazine supermodel, your clothes don't match the current trend, or you drive an old model car. It is easy to fall into the trap of comparing ourselves to other people's accomplishments.

We are social by nature and yearn for social connection and a sense of belonging. But when we compare ourselves to others, we become susceptible to mental health risks and dissatisfaction, and we lose our self-confidence. This can result in negative thoughts, high levels of anxiety and depression, and sometimes, impulse spending—buying things we don't need so we can fit in.

Comparison can steal your joy—leaving you emotionally drained and, for some people, in a financial mess, trying to keep up. Studies show that spending money just so you can keep up with the latest trends can lead to financial distress (Cruz, 2023).

This does not mean you shouldn't splurge once in a while. There's nothing wrong with buying a new pair of Louboutin shoes if it's within your budget. However, if you use your credit card to buy stuff you do not need just because it's the latest trend, you may end up neck-deep into debt and frustrated.

Be content with who you are and where you are in life while working toward achieving your dreams. Practice gratitude for what you already have and observe your contentment levels rise.

You have the power to transform your life and the ability to achieve success. When you practice self-reflection, you will begin to learn more about yourself and discover qualities you have been taking for granted that could propel you toward success in life. You will better understand your values and what is important to you and realize that you have needs that need to be fulfilled for you to function at your optimum. As you continue to develop your positive mindset, remember that every step you take each day as you follow your plan to achieve your goals leads to the realization of your vision for your life.

Chapter 4:

THE ROLE OF NEED FULFILLMENT: ALIGNING YOUR NEEDS FOR A POSITIVE MINDSET

Know what sparks the light in you.
Then, use that light to illuminate the world.
–Oprah Winfrey

Have you been searching for the secret to happiness? Perhaps you look at the people in your life and admire their ability to gracefully navigate through life—even when they are facing raging storms. Do you sometimes wish that, if life was easier and your burdens lighter, you would finally find the happiness you yearn for? Or, maybe you feel like meeting your ideal partner, landing your dream job, or buying your dream home would answer the question, "Am I ever going to find true happiness."

Everyone is searching for happiness and meaning in life. But only a few people ever realize what true happiness means.

Before we go any further, take a moment to think about what happiness means to you. In your journal, write down what a happy life looks like—to you. What activities would you participate in? How will you express your happiness, and who will benefit from it? What feelings and emotions would you develop and nurture? The answers to these questions will help you on your journey. They will help you identify your priorities and things that matter to you.

The Key to Unlocking Happiness

The key to happiness is meeting all your needs. Codependency often leads people to put other people's needs ahead of theirs and have challenges identifying, expressing, and meeting their own needs. For most people, it is easier to identify and fulfill other people's desires. In the long run, accommodating other people's needs and neglecting your own can result in a disconnection from your needs and wants. This behavior is often the result of unmet childhood needs. As children, we were subjected to meeting the needs of our parents and meeting their expectations and those of the societies we grew up in. Some people grew up in environments where—to survive a controlling parent or cope with physical and emotional unavailability, they had to pay less attention to their needs. As time progressed, they learned to tune out their needs to avoid shame and disappointment.

As a result, in adulthood, we end up sacrificing our needs and desires in relationships at the expense of our happiness. Initially, we are motivated by our love for the people in our lives, but eventually, there will be an imbalance in our relationships, and we end up resentful and discontent. If left unresolved, this pattern can result in blaming people for their selfishness—when all you need is to meet your needs.

As we grow, we must learn how to navigate through getting our needs met by others and, at the same time, meeting other people's needs. Our loved ones are important and bring joy and light into our lives. Taking care of them is an obligation and a way to show how much we love and care for them. However, if you neglect some aspects of your life, your life will feel out of balance. You might feel irritable, tired, exhausted, and even resentful.

Awareness of your expectations on how you want others to meet your needs versus how you meet other people's needs is crucial in life because your expectations impact your choices, behaviors, relationships, and contributions to the world around you.

Why Meeting Your Needs Matters

One thing that can stand in the way of productivity and personal satisfaction is not meeting your needs. Studies show that people are happier and perform better when these four basic needs are met: physical, emotional, mental, and spiritual (Schwartz and Porath, 2017). This shows that when we feel appreciated, focused, purposeful, and energized, our performance improves. For example, when you take some time to rest during a workday, and you allow yourself to reenergize, you can perform at your optimum. Being valued and appreciated builds trust and security in your relationships, which saves you from spending your time and energy seeking validation. Instead, you spend your time and channel energy toward creating more value and building meaningful relationships.

Unmet needs can cause emotional pain and dissatisfaction. You may not understand why you feel pain. But when your needs are met, you feel happier, grounded, calm, safe, focused, and loved.

Meeting your needs also

- builds a sense of contentment—you feel grateful, safe, and energized when your needs are addressed.

- lowers levels of depression, fear, loneliness, and anxiety.

- makes you feel good about yourself. When your needs are met, you feel balanced, and your health and well-being improve.

Identifying Your Needs

We all have different needs based on our values, desires, family history, identities, and personalities. For most people, it is easier to meet their physical needs than their emotional needs, especially if that was not modeled to them growing up. And sometimes, it can be a result of a lack of boundaries. Establishing healthy boundaries in your life can help you care for your needs while ensuring that you are respected and treated kindly by others. To effectively care for your needs, you must first identify them. Research shows that people who can identify their needs have a better chance of meeting them than people who don't (Panda, 2022).

Think of your life as a garden and each aspect of your life as represented by a flower. Like in a garden, you will find different kinds of flowers that bring color and beauty to your garden, and it is the same with each aspect of your life. Think of red carnations as representing your work and responsibilities, lilies as your friendships, and red roses as your romantic relationships. To care for your garden, you must water the flowers.

Watering the flowers can be compared to the time and energy you spend caring for your needs. Just like in gardening, if your water can is empty, you wouldn't leave your flowers dry and let them wither; instead, you would refill the can to continue caring for and nurturing them. It is the same with each aspect of your life. You must identify and meet your needs to gain a sense of fulfillment.

When you focus on meeting your needs and making time for the things that are important to you, doing activities that inspire creativity can boost your morale and self-esteem. This improved sense of self-worth will flow into your work and relationships. For example, you might decide to take a different career route because you want to create more family time. Or, you will finally have the courage to end a toxic relationship and focus more on your growth and development.

Taking a step back to assess your life is an opportunity to refocus on what you want and improve your life, and it requires identifying your needs. Identifying your needs involves evaluating yourself—your mind, body, and spirit, as well as your life in general. Asking yourself questions such as, "Why am I feeling like this?"; "What is happening around me?"; or "What can I do to make myself feel better?" Answering these questions can help you identify your unmet needs and find ways to fulfill them. This kind of self-care creates a balance in life. It teaches you to communicate your needs and helps you build better relationships.

One key thing to remember is that when you identify your needs, you must take steps toward fulfilling them. If you are feeling tired, then get some rest. If you feel hungry, get something to eat, and if you are not physically feeling well, seek medical attention.

This may sound easy enough, but it isn't, especially with fulfilling your emotional needs. For some people, it is difficult to seek help and learn ways to deal with their emotions, for example, anger. But the best you can do for yourself and your loved ones if you have anger issues is to seek professional help and practice anger management techniques. This can improve your communication skills and the way you interact with others and help you build healthier relationships.

Questions to Ask Yourself for Self-Focus

We often think that saying "No" to others will make us lose validation and that always saying yes will bring us joy and happiness. While we may find joy in caring for others, depending on external validation for personal satisfaction can lead to stress and frustration, and it is not an effective way to achieve mental and emotional wellness. You have the power to define your happiness.

Here are a few questions that may help you identify your needs.

- What do I enjoy doing when I'm alone?

- What am I most curious to learn, and how can I achieve this?

- Are there recurring patterns that emerge when I write down my thoughts and desires?

- Do I treat myself with the same love and respect I would treat my dearest friend?

Answering these questions will help direct your focus to the things that matter to you, independent of people.

The Different Types of Human Needs

Here are four key areas to focus on when identifying your needs:

- **Physical:** This involves taking care of your health, eating healthy foods, getting enough sleep, and exercising.

- **Emotional:** This involves practicing self-reflection, self-love, self-compassion, and emotional regulation.

- **Spiritual:** This involves doing spiritual practices such as meditation, practicing your faith, and following your life purpose, such as volunteering for a worthy cause.

- **Personal:** This involves making time to relax, maintaining healthy relationships, building financial stability, and indulging in pleasures.

To experience fulfillment in life, you must ensure that all your needs are met. Abraham Maslow's Hierarchy of Needs sheds light on the impact of the five basic human needs on personal growth (Roguska, 2021), which are:

- physiological

- safety

- love and belongingness

- esteem

- self-actualization

Maslow's Hierarchy of Needs provides insights into human motivation based on seeking change and satisfaction through personal growth (Roguska, 2021).

According to Maslow, our needs fluctuate at different times during the process of our growth and development—with some needs taking precedence over others.

Maslow's Five Basic Human Needs

Physiological Needs

At the bottom of Maslow's Hierarchy of Needs are physiological needs. These are needs we need for survival, such as food, shelter, clothing, water, air, warmth, and sleep. Failure to meet these needs often results in physical illness, mental health illness, emotional distress, and negative behavior patterns.

It is important to care for the needs at the bottom of the hierarchy before attending to the ones at the top.

Safety and Security

The need to feel safe and secure is critical in our development. This includes protection against violence and theft, emotional stability, financial and job security, health insurance, and well-being. We meet our safety and security needs when we pay our bills, ensure that we have a roof above our heads, build healthy relationships, and have jobs to help us honor our financial obligations.

Meeting these needs is essential to your survival; however, it must be balanced with meeting other needs to achieve self-actualization. For example, when applying for a job, you want to land not only a job that will provide financial and career stability but also one that provides meaningful opportunities, adequate compensation, and a possibility for career advancement.

To add on, adequate housing provides safety, support, and stability, which is key to survival.

Love and Belonging

This is the third need in Maslow's Hierarchy of Needs, and it involves social connection and acceptance. We have a natural desire to be loved, supported, secure, and to be in companionship. A newborn baby, for instance, relies on his or her mother to meet their needs. The bond between mother and child fulfills the need to form a close relationship for both parties.

We meet the need to be loved and accepted by developing meaningful relationships. It is possible to build a strong connection with friends, partners, and family and build a stable social network.

Esteem

Esteem needs address feelings of worth and respect gained from achievement and recognition. Esteem needs refer to respect for others and the need to feel respected by others. Wisdom and knowledge are key to satisfying the need for recognition.

Meeting esteem needs makes us feel appreciated and accepted, and when they are not met, we feel inferior, hopeless, weak, and helpless.

It is crucial to have autonomy and control over your life to fulfill your esteem needs, and this requires self-determination and freedom.

Self-Actualization

Abraham Maslow's definition of self-actualization is "becoming everything you are capable of becoming"(Raypole, 2020). In other words, it is the ability to become the best version of yourself. Masow's Hierarchy of Needs provides insight into how we can achieve self-actualization by fulfilling the four basic needs first.

There are different characteristics associated with self-actualization. These include:

- **Creativity:** Self-actualization inspires creativity and enables you to seek effective solutions to challenges in a different way than what most people would do.

- **Living independently:** When you realize your potential, you live your life free from other people's opinions, and you are not ashamed to express your individuality.

- **Being truthful and realistic:** Part of growth is living truthfully and with realistic expectations. This makes you feel grounded and in tune with actual possibilities. You can easily sense people who are not being truthful.

- **Enjoying peak experiences:** When you achieve self-actualization, you experience a feeling of connectedness that comes with eye-opening moments of wonder and joy. For example, when you help others, you feel a sense of joy and fulfillment.

- **Focusing on the bigger picture.** Self-actualization can inspire you to consider others and not just yourself. You develop a passion to be part of something bigger and significant, such as participating in a cause, mission, or purpose.

- **Embracing the unknown:** The need for certainty causes most people to procrastinate and not realize their potential. Self-actualization enables you to embrace the unknown and forge a way forward, even if you do not know what the future holds.

- **Building meaningful relationships:** Growth comes with many changes, including your relationships. Self-actualized people would rather have long-lasting relationships with a few people than casual friendships with a lot of people.

Remember, growth is a process. If you live with authenticity, follow your purpose, and show genuine concern for others, you are well on your way to realizing self-actualization.

The Six Core Emotional Needs

Emotional needs have a significant impact on our lives, whether we realize it or not. They are feelings and conditions we need to feel satisfied and at peace. Failure to fulfill them often leads to frustration and dissatisfaction. Examples of emotional needs include feelings of accomplishment, feeling appreciated, being safe, and being part of a community.

As humans, we need emotional nourishment the same way we need air, food, and water; therefore, emotional needs are crucial to our growth and development. They are deep-rooted and unique to each of us and influence the decisions we make in our lives.

Emotional needs are based on your identity, upbringing, beliefs, experiences, values, and genetic predisposition. Fulfilling them can help you make better decisions in your life.

To identify your emotional needs, you must understand your emotions. Take some time to reflect on how your emotions have impacted your life and influenced your thoughts, feelings, behaviors, as well as your decisions. For example, if, growing up, you were shamed for expressing your emotions, you may have learned to keep your feelings to yourself, even as an adult. Therefore, identifying and caring for your needs is crucial in your development and how you interact with the world around you.

To understand human needs and motivations better, research has further broken down the five basic human needs to help us realize our potential (Roguska, 2021).

- **Certainty:** This refers to the need to feel safe and the ability to adapt and cope with change. When this need is unmet, we often feel insecure, worried, and stressed.

- **Variety:** This relates to our experiences, ideas, and outlooks throughout life. Fulfilling the need for variety allows us to explore new possibilities and understand the world around us better. Finding a balance between rules, regulations, processes, and norms, as well as stepping out of your comfort zone can help you practice variety.

- **Significance:** This refers to having a purpose and sense of meaning and value in life. Significance is a result of having internal knowledge, being honest, and expressing your individuality to the world. To fulfill this need, you must be comfortable pursuing passions outside of the ordinary life and surrounding yourself with people who uplift and support you. Participating in meaningful activities, such as volunteering for a worthy cause, can also help you feel significant.

- **Love and connection:** This is your need to feel connected with other people. It involves building positive and secure relationships with loved ones and social circles. We express love and mutual acceptance through affection, closeness, and tolerance. The ability to love, accept, validate, understand, and relate with yourself and others is key to nurturing relationships.

- **Growth:** This involves developing your potential and capabilities. Growth involves adaptability and embracing current situations while working on your future goals. Growth also requires patience and hard work for us to achieve self-fulfillment.

- **Contribution:** This refers to giving. It could be your time, skills, energy, or resources. Giving adds purpose and meaning to your life. There are many ways you can contribute to your family, community, and the world at large. For example, helping someone in need, giving financial aid to a charity, or teaching children to read. Helping others makes us feel like we are part of something bigger. When you focus less on what you will gain from your contribution and more on serving others, life becomes more fulfilling, and you feel more connected to others.

As you learn to refocus on yourself, remember there are many aspects of your life, and each has its own needs, so treat yourself as your whole self.

Practical Ways to Tend to Your Needs

Self-care is crucial to human development and our overall success. When we do not tend to our needs, we often get overwhelmed, frustrated, and disconnected from ourselves. Lack of boundaries, fear of appearing selfish, and being a people pleaser can cause you to neglect your needs while you are fulfilling the needs of others.

While taking care of others is a noble thing to do, failure to tend to your own needs often results in resentment, dissatisfaction, deterioration in health, and mental health issues.

The good news is that there are practical ways you can incorporate into your daily routine that can help you focus on yourself, and if it feels uncomfortable at first, remember that developing a new habit requires time and consistency.

Here are a few practical ways to help you tend to your needs that you can begin with:

- **Set aside time for yourself:** You are allowed to take time for yourself. Making time to do the activities you love inspires creativity and reenergizes you. Are you a nature lover? Go for a hike or picnic and connect with Mother Nature. Are you an adrenaline junkie? Do an intense workout or go surfing. Participate in activities that make you feel alive. And if spending some alone time means staying at home and watching movies or playing video games, then do it, and do not be ashamed.

- **Set clear boundaries:** Boundaries are an important part of building healthy relationships. It can be an effective way to teach people how you want to be treated. For example, if you dedicate your evenings to family time, let your co-workers know that after 6 p.m., you will not be taking work-related phone calls. Or, if you are invited to a party on Friday night and you have plans to spend some alone time and rest, you may politely decline the invite by saying, "Thank you for inviting me, but I have plans for tonight. Rain check?" Often, people won't hold that against you, and you will be able to honor your commitment to yourself.

67

- **Keep a Journal:** Journaling is an excellent self-reflection tool that can enhance your mental and emotional well-being. Writing your thoughts in a notebook or journal can ease anxiety and help you process your emotions. You can understand your feelings better and learn to let go of the negative ones. Journaling can also help you identify what you need. For example, if you feel overwhelmed, writing your feelings down can help you get to the root of what is causing those feelings. It clears your mind, and you gain a new perspective on your life.

- **Practice self-evaluation:** Meeting your needs requires you to take some time to assess your life. We live in a fast-paced world, and it is easy to get caught up in running errands and lose sight of the things that are valuable to you. Checking in with yourself from time to time ensures that you take care of yourself physically and mentally. Make time to pause, breathe, and listen to how you feel. This allows you to get in touch with your true feelings and needs, and you can achieve this through practicing mindfulness and meditation, as well as listening to your intuition.

- **Actively choose you:** Fulfilling your needs requires you to constantly choose yourself. Pursue the things that inspire, satisfy, and make you happy. It could be spending time in nature or playing sports. If you love dancing, attend a music concert. Do what you love and what you are good at while ensuring that you listen to your soul because it knows how best you can honor yourself.

- **Be familiar with your inner voice:** Meeting your needs involves getting acquainted with your inner voice. It is when you start listening to your inner voice that you can build a relationship with yourself because your inner self knows your deep-rooted desires and what you need to fulfill them.

Focusing on yourself and meeting your needs is not a selfish thing to do. Instead, it is the best thing you can do yourself and for your relationships. Often, society deems focusing on oneself as selfishness and commends those who are caring, giving, noble, selfless, and forgiving, but these traits are what we can do for others, and we cannot take care of others when we cannot take care of ourselves. You are as important as everyone else, and to live a fulfilling life, your needs must be met.

Developing a positive mindset involves practicing gratitude for what you already have. However, this can be difficult when you feel a sense of lack associated with not tending to your needs. Therefore, focusing on your needs is crucial for your survival and overall success. When you are grateful, you attract more things to be grateful for.

Chapter 5

LIVING IN GRATITUDE:
THE ROLE OF GRATITUDE'S
IN POSITIVITY

Each day comes bearing its gifts.
Untie the ribbon. –Ann Ruth Schabacker

What are you grateful for today? Why are you grateful for it? And "How has practicing gratitude impacted your emotions and your life?"

We often get caught up in trying to figure out our lives. We set goals and targets for our careers, we have expectations of how we want to be treated in relationships, and we follow the latest trends and social media influencers who, for most people, define what a happy life looks like. For some people, living a happy life means being free of debt, driving a luxurious Mercedes-Benz S-Class, or owning a lavish modern home with elegant furnishings in a serene neighborhood with stunning views. For some, living a simple life in the countryside with their families—surrounded by their friends and nature defines a happy life.

The bottom line is that we all want to be happy. But what is happiness?

Happiness is an emotional state characterized by feelings of fulfillment, achievement, contribution, and gratification. We have different ways to define a happy life based on our values, interests, and upbringing. When people talk about the true meaning of happiness, they are either referring to how they feel in the present moment or in a general sense of how they feel about life. Whatever your definition may be, happiness is a vital emotion that can increase self-confidence and self-esteem.

While happiness has different definitions, it is often associated with positive emotions and life satisfaction, and some of the signs of happiness include:

- feeling optimistic and that the conditions of your life are good.

- feeling that you have achieved what you want in life.

- being flexible, going with the flow, and allowing life to take its course.

- practicing self-care and being compassionate to yourself.

- gaining a sense of meaning and purpose in life.

- wanting to share your joy with others.

- feeling grateful.

One thing to note is that happiness does not refer to a state of euphoria; instead, it is a feeling of experiencing more positive emotions than negative ones.

When you are truly happy, you experience gratitude, not only for the huge accomplishments but for tiny things as well, like the sun shining through your window in the morning, the lady who was kind enough to help you at the grocery store, or the waiter who serves you coffee everyone morning, with a smile, at your favorite coffee shop. All these tiny things add up with time to condition your mind to notice the positive things life offers. When you start noticing the good that already exists in your life, you can cultivate an attitude of gratitude. And gratitude and positivity are linked.

Developing the ability to be grateful is not difficult; however, it does take practice. The more you focus on the things you are grateful for, the easier it will be to notice more blessings to be grateful for.

Why Gratitude Is Important

Living in today's world, where media measures success by a person's financial and social status, can make it difficult to feel grateful for what you have. You look all around you, and everyone seems to be thriving and has it all, more so the people all over social media platforms like Facebook, Instagram, Twitter, and YouTube, to name a few. Often, we find ourselves comparing ourselves to social media influencers and celebrities, and if we feel like we haven't achieved something significant in life, we get frustrated. We work hard, and sometimes, just to fit the world's definition of a successful person. We follow trends and buy things we don't necessarily need—which often leaves people in financial distress.

Trying to fit in can create a gap between who you envision yourself to be and who the world thinks you are. You spend your time trying to blend in with the rest of the world such that you end up losing sight of your values and your essence.

Practicing gratitude conditions your mind to focus on positive feelings, emotions, and events in your life. It promotes good behavior and can change your perception of yourself and your outlook on life.

Here are a few more benefits of practicing gratitude and how it can enhance your well-being.

Increases Immunity

Gratitude can have significant lasting effects on your health and well-being. It can improve immune functioning and your quality of sleep, as well as lower blood pressure. Studies show that grateful people have better heart health, less inflammation, and healthier heart rhythms (Prange-Morgan, 2022).

There is a link between our minds and our bodies. When we maintain a positive mindset, we can develop healthy coping strategies, build healthier habits, and feel better about ourselves. This has an impact on our physical health. When we have a positive view of our medical care, we are more likely to get the results we desire and efficiently recover from diseases (7 Ways to Boost Your Health by Practicing Gratitude, 2023). For example, in 19 studies involving nearly 3,000 participants, researchers found that gratitude not only promotes mental health and more sustainable healthy habits but also a healthier heart (Wang and Song, 2023).

Living intentionally can help you identify even the tiniest things to be thankful for every day. When you develop the habit of noticing the blessing you already have, you feel good about yourself and the world around you, and you can create a better life for yourself.

Improves Memory and Reduces Chances of Cognitive Deterioration with Age

Thanking yourself, others, Mother Nature, or the Almighty in any form can enlighten the mind and enhance our happiness. Studies show that the root causes of mental health disorders, such as anxiety and depression, are a result of unhappiness (Chowdhury, 2019).

The benefits of practicing gratitude may not be seen immediately, but you will begin to notice changes over time.

Practicing gratitude builds resilience and reduces the negative effects of stress. Chronic stress does not only affect cardiovascular function but brain function as well. Positive psychology can be useful in increasing the life span of elderly people and mitigating emotional health disorders present at different stages of life through strategies that promote positive emotions, cognitions, and behaviors (Chamorro-Garrido et al., 2021).

Memories from personal experiences play a vital role in our well-being. Remembering the past can bring positive emotions, and gratitude magnifies good memories from the past, which in turn increases life satisfaction.

Improves Sleep Quality and Decreases Insomnia

Gratitude may ease the negative effects of stress partly by improving the quality of sleep and preventing insomnia. Cardiovascular function and sleep quality are important in maintaining a healthy brain.

Research shows that receiving and showing simple acts of kindness activates the hypothalamus—the hormone that regulates body temperature, heart rate, hunger, and the sleep-wake cycle. It is also responsible for releasing dopamine (the hormone that gives pleasure and motivation). This, therefore, regulates all bodily functions controlled by the hypothalamus, of which sleep is a vital one (Chowdhury, 2019).

Hypothalamic regulation triggered by gratitude promotes deeper sleep naturally, and when it is not working properly, it can cause problems in the body that result in a wide range of disorders, such as insomnia, increased or decreased appetite, malnutrition, infertility, and infections, to name a few. When you are filled with gratitude and positivity, you are more likely to sleep better and wake up feeling refreshed and energetic every morning.

Decreases Ongoing Pain and Discomfort

A study conducted on evaluating the effect of gratitude on physical well-being shows that 16 percent of the patients who kept a gratitude journal reported reduced pain symptoms and were more willing to exercise and cooperate with the treatment procedure. More research into the cause revealed that by regulating the level of dopamine, gratitude fills us with more vitality, thereby reducing subjective feelings of pain (Chowdhury, 2019).

Another study conducted in 2019 on the effects of gratitude journaling in managing pain and disability for adults with arthritis suggests that self-directed gratitude journaling effectively reduces the fear of movement, pain anxiety, and pain efficacy (Datta, 2023).

The fear of movement and pain anxiety are common emotions experienced by chronic pain patients, especially those involved in accidents or injuries, and can be all-consuming. Together, they can form a repetitive chronic pain cycle.

Practicing gratitude journaling can significantly improve pain anxiety, fear of movement, and pain efficacy and interrupt the pain cycle.

Reduces Body Inflammation

Among other health conditions, chronic stress can cause body inflammation. Feeling grateful and appreciating others for what they do for us releases good hormones and improves the functioning of the immune system.

The results of a study conducted on cardiovascular health show that individuals with a habit of practicing gratitude exhibited lower incidences of inflammation, while individuals with heart disease who cultivated gratitude experienced less inflammation and better vascular function (Cousin et al. 2020).

This shows us the importance of being thankful and how it impacts our health and well-being.

Improves Your Mental Well-Being

Have you ever wondered why some people seem happier than others? Could it be because of their achievements, or are they simply born with the ability to be happy, even when they go through the storms in this life? What does true happiness mean, and is it achievable?

Perhaps you may be thinking that accomplishing all your heart's desires could be the answer to these questions, but it is not. You do not have to have everything you desire to be happy and feel grateful. The stress and anxiety of trying to keep up with the latest trends and chasing success can prevent you from living in the moment, embracing your current circumstances, and experiencing the blessings that surround you.

Practicing gratitude when you feel stressed and uncertain about the future can have a positive impact on your emotions, which can improve your physical health. Studies show that when we think about what we appreciate, the calming part of the nervous system—which has protective benefits for the body, is triggered. This increases oxytocin (the love hormone responsible for social bonding) and decreases cortisol (the stress hormone) (Maidenberg, 2020).

Results of a study conducted on participants who showed appreciation revealed that those who practiced gratitude had lower levels of cortisol, improved cardiac functioning, and developed when faced with challenges and emotional setbacks (McCraty, 2002).

This shows that gratitude can reduce symptoms of anxiety and depression. By practicing gratitude, we can reduce stress levels and rewire the brain to handle stressful situations with flexibility and awareness.

Enhances Self-Assurance and Decreases Rage, Jealousy, and Envy

Self-confidence enables us to deal with challenges, take risks, and embrace the opportunities life offers us. Gratitude is a confidence booster. Cultivating thankfulness can enhance self-assurance and personal growth.

Gratitude is more than just saying "Thank you." It is one of the most effective ways for transformation and can change your perception of yourself and the world around you.

Here are a few more reasons why gratitude can boost your self-confidence and reduce rage, envy, and jealousy:

- **It can help you develop a positive self-image:** Gratitude encourages you to focus on your positive traits rather than dwelling on negative ones. Being thankful for what you already have and acknowledging your accomplishments can help you realize your worth and boost your self-esteem.

- **It helps overcome self-doubt:** Confidence often decreases when we doubt ourselves. Gratitude reminds you of past victories and the support you received from others, which promotes self-assurance that can help you overcome self-doubt.

- **It enables you to embrace challenges:** Grateful people often view challenges as opportunities to learn and grow rather than as obstacles. This shift in mindset

79

enables you to tackle challenges with confidence and with an open mind to learn from them.

- **It fosters a positive mindset:** Practicing gratitude increases happiness and resilience and can help you build strong interpersonal relationships. It involves cultivating a positive attitude toward life and people. When you are grateful for what you have and acknowledge and accept where you are in life—while working on your goals, you prevent measuring your success against other people's achievements.

By cultivating a grateful attitude, you can celebrate other people's success without holding back or feeling envious of them. Practicing gratitude does not require you to have everything you desire. It involves noticing the tiny blessings that surround you. You become mindful of your surroundings and attract more blessings to be thankful for.

What Is a Gratitude Practice?

To experience the health benefits of gratitude, creating a gratitude practice routine is key. Practicing gratitude isn't a difficult task to do: The challenging part can be finding the right time and committing to doing it regularly.

There are many gratitude exercises you can practice daily. You can either set aside time each day to reflect on what you are grateful for in your life or write in your journal the people, interactions, events, and all other things you appreciate. Let your creative genius guide you. Perhaps you find it easier to practice gratitude by showing others how much you appreciate them. You could leave them a note or text message or call them to let them know how grateful you are to have them in your life.

Maybe you are wondering, "What if I struggle to identify things to be grateful for?" Well, everyone experiences blessings each day; try not to fixate your mind on huge victories or huge events in your life, but start by noticing the tiny things that surround you. For example, the sun rays shining through your bedroom window in the morning, waking up next to the person you love, being a parent to wonderful and respectful children, and the home you live in that shelters you and provides protection.

Identify the things that give you a sense of meaning and purpose. You will be amazed at how it will change your perspective on life.

Remember, there is no wrong way to start your daily gratitude practice. For starters, consider your daily schedule and designate specific times of the day for your gratitude practice. Next, find a quiet space where you will do your practice every day. You could create a sacred space in your home—whether you decide to use the entire room, a corner in your room, or your garden for your daily practices, it is entirely up to you. What is important is that you find a quiet space where you will feel comfortable and not be disturbed while practicing self-reflection.

Doing your practices in the same place every day can help reinforce the habit.

How to Practice Gratitude Daily

A lifestyle change can be intimidating at first attempt. It takes time and great effort to develop new habits, introduce a completely new way of thinking, and hold yourself accountable daily for making the changes you desire. If you do not see the results immediately, do not be disheartened. I guarantee you that your efforts will pay off in the long run. Be patient with yourself and understand that you do not have to have everything you desire to practice gratitude. , nor do you need to do it perfectly. Give yourself time to fully learn the techniques that are most effective for you to cultivate appreciation.

Additionally, you can find a community of like-minded people who have similar goals to yours—who will support and hold you accountable.

Even though you might not know where to begin initially, making tiny adjustments along the way is a step in the right way. Here are a few gratitude exercises you can add to your daily routine to help you cultivate an attitude of gratitude.

Make a List of What You are Grateful For

We often celebrate the major events that take place in our lives, such as accomplishing something huge like landing a promotion at work, purchasing a new home or car, getting married, the birth of a child into the family, birthdays, and school graduations. These major life events are significant to us because they occur once in a while. It is also important to acknowledge and appreciate the tiny daily occurrences. One way to do this is to think of all the things you did the previous day. Make a list of the events, people, or interactions you are grateful for.

To take it further, identify commonalities on your list. Are there events that repeat every day or weekly? How many of those are big events?

Remember to acknowledge yourself as well. What can you appreciate yourself for? Your body, mind, or spirit? If you struggle with being grateful to yourself, perhaps you can start with a self-compassion exercise. We will learn more about how you can turn self-criticism into self-compassion in detail in Chapter 6.

Thank Your Loved Ones and Those Who Extend Kindness to You

One of the many ways to practice gratitude is to appreciate the people who extend kindness toward you. Thank people for their support, love, help, and presence. If a friend offers to babysit while you work, thank them for taking the time to help you. And if a colleague or your entire team helps you work on an important project in your organization, show them how grateful you are. Thank them for their team effort and dedication to making the project a success. Thank the waitress who serves you food at the restaurant or the bartender who serves you drinks after a long day juggling work commitment. You can leave them a thank you note or buy them a gift. And if it is your loved ones, call or text them; however, you want to show your appreciation, do it and watch how good you feel afterward.

Reframe Your Thoughts

Practicing gratitude can help you notice opportunities and give you the confidence to take advantage of the opportunities when they present themselves. You must look creatively for new situations and circumstances that will lead to feelings of satisfaction and give you more reasons to be grateful, and you can achieve this by reframing your thoughts and cultivating positivity.

Appreciate Your Community

It is important to ensure that you cultivate and normalize the culture of gratitude in your home and community. People tend to be influenced by the behaviors and attitudes of those they hold in high regard. If you want to experience more gratitude at home, school, church, or place of work, start by appreciating your community.

For example, if you run or manage a business, provide opportunities for your team to give thanks to each other. You can have weekly team meetings where you acknowledge teammates for their work. To show appreciation to the community you live in, you could serve at a center for the elderly and donate food, clothes, blankets, toys, and other items you no longer use at home to the less fortunate.

Spread kindness by performing acts of kindness. Hold the door for someone, teach young kids to read, or bake some cookies for the new folks in your neighborhood. Remember, even the tiniest act of kindness can make a difference in your community.

Focus on Self-Reflection

Gratitude encourages self-reflection and introspection. It allows us to gain insight into our thoughts, feelings, emotions, and values. By intentionally expressing gratitude for our experiences and relationships, we gain a deeper understanding of ourselves.

Cultivating a grateful attitude is a skill that can be learned and reinforced with mindfulness practice. When you take time to pause, be in the present moment, and notice all that you have, you can instantly stir up feelings of gratitude.

By acknowledging and appreciating the positive aspects of our lives, we become more attuned to our strengths and emotions and can recognize areas we need to improve on. This heightened sense of self-awareness empowers us to make conscious choices aligned with our true selves and be satisfied with our lives.

Through practicing mindfulness and self-reflection, you can become more aware of your environment and daily activities, which makes it easier to notice more things to be grateful for every day.

Journal With Intention

Journaling is a powerful self-reflection exercise, and it's even extremely beneficial if you journal with intention. Intentional journaling involves setting an intention for your writing. What do you want to write about? Is there a specific topic or goal you want to focus on?

Journaling with intention can bring about positive outcomes, and sometimes, the outcome can simply be developing self-awareness or helping you make important decisions and setting very specific goals. You can also use journaling to improve your problem-solving skills and to manage stress or difficult emotions.

Studies show that maintaining a journal can help us acknowledge and accept our circumstances rather than judge—which often results in negative emotions in reaction to stressful situations (Connors, 2023). Journaling also has a positive impact on our mental health. It can significantly reduce levels of stress and improve cognitive processes (Brennan, 2021).

Practicing journaling regularly can help you gain insight into your emotions, behaviors, and thought patterns and enable you to change those that no longer serve you.

Here are a few ideas on how you can begin practicing intentional journaling.

- **Set an intention:** Decide what you want to focus on in your journaling. To help you with this task, take some time to answer the following questions:

  - Why do you want to start journaling?

  - Is there a specific topic you want to write about?

  - How often do you plan to journal?

  - What do you hope to achieve from journaling?

Setting clear intentions and objectives is crucial before you get to the next steps of your journaling process.

- **Create a journaling routine:** It's easy to write on days when you feel inspired and motivated, but what about when you are not? Creating a journaling routine can help you stay focused, even on days when you feel uninspired to write. For example, you can set aside five to ten minutes every morning when you wake up or every evening before bedtime for your journaling practice. Setting a routine allows you to prioritize journaling and eventually form a habit.

- **Find a journaling technique that suits you:** At first, journaling can be daunting, but remember, there is no right or wrong way of doing it. Your journal should be whatever you want it to be–whether you choose to express your thoughts, reflect on the day, or for self-reflection. Keeping a paper journal is one way you can start journaling. While it can help you develop and express your ideas more clearly, it is not the only method of journaling. Find A method that works best for you. Perhaps using a laptop, phone, or tablet makes journaling more enjoyable for you. You do not have to limit yourself to one method. For example, if you prefer writing in a paper journal but suddenly get a burst of inspiration while commuting on the subway, the best thing to do would be to use the notes app on your phone to write down your thoughts before you forget them.

- **Start your journaling by practicing gratitude:** One way to start journaling with intention is to start by expressing gratitude. Make a list of the things you are grateful for. This is a powerful way to create a positive atmosphere. It is easy to lose sight of your blessings when you are focused on the bad things happening around you. Being thankful creates more opportunities to be grateful and can stir up feelings of peace, love, and kindness. You feel more relaxed and ready to move on to other, setting your goals.

- **Let go of judgments:** When journaling, it is crucial to practice self-compassion and not allow your inner critic to take over. Journaling is a judgment-free zone— a space where you can be free to express yourself. Remember, your journal is for your eyes only. Therefore, there is no need to feel embarrassed or ashamed. When you are self-critical or afraid that someone might read your journal, you might hold back from truly expressing your authenticity and honesty.

- **Set realistic expectations:** When you start journaling, do not expect to write a lot of pages filled with insightful thoughts. Be realistic. If you set aside five to ten minutes of your time each day to write on just one topic, say you want to focus on your personal goals, focus on that. It will be enough for that day or journaling session. Having unrealistic expectations can be discouraging and can cause you to lose inspiration if you do not see progress. Like any other habit, journaling requires setting realistic and attainable goals and taking small steps each day to achieve your desired results.

- **Use journal prompts.** There may be days when you find yourself staring at your journal and thinking, "What should I write about today?" Worry not. You can use journaling prompts to help you overcome writer's block. Here is a list of things to write about on days when you feel less inspired:

○ List the things and people you are thankful for.

○ Write daily positive affirmations. It could be statements like "I am grateful that I am healthy" or " I am proud of who I am and who I am becoming."

○ Write about a recent situation that challenged you.

○ Journal the things that bring you joy each day.

○ Write about the best decision you have ever made.

○ Write an (unsent) letter to someone in your life or from your past.

Journaling is a therapeutic and healing exercise that allows you to be completely vulnerable and honest with yourself while creating a safe space to process your thoughts. Besides helping you process your thoughts; journaling can clear mental clutter. It allows you to reflect on deeper concepts that you often pay less attention to.

Create Gratitude Rituals.

A gratitude ritual is a practice whereby you tap into an attitude of gratitude. There are different types of gratitude rituals you can try.

Here are some rituals you can begin with:

1. In your journal, list five things you are grateful for in a journal. These can be significant or tiny blessings that surround you. Consider doing this first thing in the morning and before bedtime. Appreciate the good

that is happening around you and watch your positivity increase.

2. When you are facing a challenge during the day and need to shift back into a positive mindset, slow down and take a moment to breathe. Look for at least one thing you can be grateful for.

3. Keep a gratitude jar or box. When you feel grateful, write down what you are grateful for on a piece of paper and put it inside the jar. At the end of the month, pull out all the papers and read the things you are grateful for.

4. Before eating a meal, take a moment to appreciate the food in front of you. Take in the colors and the aroma; take each bite slowly and savor the taste. Note what you appreciate most about the food you are about to eat. For example, you could be grateful that you have food that will nourish your body.

5. Each day, share the things you are thankful for in your life with a friend or family member.

6. Every month, write a letter to someone who has positively impacted your life.

Like most skills, gratitude can be learned and developed with time. Our brains can be trained to repeat patterns. For example, worrying about negative outcomes all the time unconsciously wires the brain to process negative information most of the time. By practicing gratitude, you can reprogram your mind to focus more on the good that is happening around you.

One of the most effective ways to practice gratitude is to reframe your thoughts from negative self-criticism to self-acceptance, and you can do this by practicing self-compassion. Let us explore how you can stop self-criticism and develop self-acceptance so that you can genuinely practice gratitude daily.

Chapter 6

From Self-Criticism to Self-Compassion

Don't waste a minute not being happy. If one window closes, run to the next window—or break down a door. –Brooke Shields

How often do you find yourself saying things like, "I'm so stupid. Why did I say that?" Or, "I'm so mad at myself for eating that slice of cake." If a friend or a family member said the same words to you while venting, how would you respond? Chances are you'd offer empathy, compassion, and understanding. Rather than criticize them, you'd reassure them that everything would be alright and that they should not be hard on themselves. You'd offer them comfort and support and let them know that mistakes are all part of learning and can help them grow.

However, many times, when these negative thoughts creep into our minds and are directed at us, we struggle to extend the same kindness and compassion we give to others to ourselves. Instead of encouraging ourselves to do better, we allow the inner critic to take over—we judge and discourage ourselves.

But rather than be judgmental, we can do justice to ourselves and practice self-compassion, even more on days when the inner voice is relentless and downright rude. When your inner critic takes over, it hurts. It does not make you feel good about yourself and rarely helps you improve your performance. It can also kill your curiosity and passion, making it difficult to sustain effort over time.

This happens to most people. We all have a harsh inner critic buried deep within us that usually shows up unconsciously. Sometimes, it can be ruthless, but you do not have to accept these negative thoughts, and you can certainly choose to change them and turn them into positive ones at any point in your life.

Silencing your inner critic is a sign of strength. It takes self-compassion and self-acceptance to overcome negative self-talk. Self-compassion is the idea of being as kind and caring to yourself as you would be to others. When you practice self-compassion, you turn down the voice of the inner critic, and this is a huge step toward developing more focus and effectiveness.

To start your journey toward personal growth, you should understand what self-criticism is and where it stems from.

Self-Criticism

The word criticism is similar to the words opinion, judgment, or assessment. Self-criticism means judging yourself or evaluating your actions, work, or performance. It involves evaluating yourself negatively, which often leads to feelings of worthlessness, guilt, and failure.

Self-criticism can be a result of your experiences in early relationships growing up. A tendency to self-criticize can be a result of:

- being raised by strict parents

- having demanding teachers or bosses

- peer pressure at school

- or competitive sporting activities.

It can also stem from your learned behaviors. For example, pursuing perfection or academic excellence can lead to a relentless inner critic. Or putting pressure on yourself to find a romantic relationship can result in low self-esteem.

This behavior can be demanding, and it has an impact on your mental health and well-being. This, however, does not mean viewing your self-criticism as a personality trait despite how it started. You are not defined by how you treat yourself. And your identity does not depend on your inner dialogue.

Shifting from self-criticism can be a challenging thing to do, but it is not impossible. It takes a lot of work, and sometimes, you might need a trained therapist to help you overcome negative thinking and negative self-talk. Therefore, if you need help, do not be ashamed to seek therapy.

What Is Self-Compassion?

Self-compassion is the ability to notice and be moved by your suffering, leading you to take action to relieve your suffering. It involves understanding that though you make mistakes, your mistakes or failures do not define you as a person, and rather than beat yourself up, embrace your imperfections, learn from your mistakes and failures, and keep growing.

We know the inner critic all too well—that critical subtitle to every action you take that says, "You don't deserve success,"

"You're a huge failure," or "Pull yourself together, you're losing it." While there are moments when we may be aware of how we speak to ourselves, often, we are unaware of the impact these negative thoughts have on us, and before we know it, we rush from task to task with a general sense of unease and anxiety.

Would it not be better to speak to yourself with the same respect, honesty, and kindness as a close friend or mentor would do when they want to support your growth?

Self-compassion brings you closer not only to yourself but also to others. You gain a better understanding that, just like other human beings, you make mistakes, go through adverse times, and experience difficult emotions that lead you to act in ways you often regret later.

Why Is Self-Compassion So Important?

Forgiving and nurturing yourself have amazing benefits for your overall well-being. Practicing self-compassion can promote better physical and mental health and healthy relationships. Studies have revealed several benefits of self-compassion, and lower levels of anxiety and depression have been observed in people with higher self-compassion (Harvard Health Publishing, 2021).

Self-compassionate people recognize when they are suffering and are kind to themselves during that period. This enables them to better care for themselves, thereby lowering their levels of anxiety and depression. Psychologist Kristin Neff's research on the idea of self-compassion revealed that one of the most effective ways to build resilience and improve our mental well-being is through self-compassion (*4 Techniques for Practicing Self-Compassion,* 2023). Instead of seeing setbacks as obstacles and something to criticize, we can cultivate compassion and bounce back from failure, and in the process, lower levels of depression, anxiety, and rumination.

Practicing self-compassion can increase your motivation and help you reach your goals. Therefore, self-compassion can be a powerful tool to help you achieve your personal goals—even if you fail a couple of times along the way.

The Components of Self-Compassion

There are three components of self-compassion (*4 Techniques for Practicing Self-Compassion,* 2023):

1. **Mindfulness:** A lack of self-awareness and understanding of what is going on with you makes it difficult to create room for your feelings. Failure to accommodate your feelings makes it impossible to practice self-compassion because we are unaware of where you are psychologically and emotionally. And if you do not know where you are, you may not know what you need. So, the idea of being fully present—mind and body, is an essential part of self-compassion.

97

2. **Self-kindness:** This focuses on self-talk and how we deal with the inner critic. The way you respond to yourself is often different from the way you respond to other people. Self-kindness is about giving yourself kindness and positive self-talk as you would others.

3. **Common humanity:** This involves realizing and accepting that it is impossible not to experience difficult periods in our lives and that challenges are part of the human experience. While our experiences may be different, everyone goes through pain and suffering at some point in their lives. This is a crucial part of developing compassion because it creates a sense of connectivity contrary to isolation.

Myths and Misconceptions About Self-Compassion

There are many misconceptions about self-compassion. Often, people are afraid to spend time in self-reflection for fear of facing their dark side. However, the best way to achieve self-awareness and acceptance is through self-reflection. Assessing your life from time to time can help you identify your behavior patterns and how you can overcome the negative ones.

To effectively do self-assessment, practicing self-compassion plays a key role. It allows you to evaluate yourself with less judgment and criticism. There are common misconceptions that keep people from being compassionate with themselves, partly because they fear that they may be seen as wallowing in self-pity, which is not the case.

Self-compassion and self-love work together to help you develop a healthy self-image.

Now, let us look at a few common myths about practicing self-compassion.

- **Self-compassion is self-pity:** Some people believe that practicing self-compassion is the same as wallowing in self-pity, but there is a huge difference between the two. Self-pity involves seeing yourself as a victim. It relies on external rescue. On the other hand, self-compassion involves acknowledging your struggles and finding effective ways to cope with challenges and improve. Practicing self-compassion enables us to deal with challenges with understanding and emotional resilience.

- **Self-compassion is self-excuse:** Another misconception about self-compassion is that if we are compassionate with ourselves, we will justify our negative behaviors rather than take responsibility. However, self-compassionate people often apologize when their behavior has done damage to others. They tend to be more committed to changing their behavior and not repeat it. In other words, self-compassion can strengthen accountability.

- **Self-compassion is self-serving:** Another common myth about self-compassion is that caring more for yourself is selfish. On the contrary, caring for yourself shows that you love yourself. And it is only when you love yourself that you can love others. Research shows that self-compassionate people have better romantic relationships (Graebner, 2021). According to research conducted by Kristin Neff and Natasha Beretvas, self-

99

compassionate people were found to be more caring, more affectionate, and considerate according to their partners (Neff and Beretvas, 2013) Participants who practiced self-compassion were also found to be more accepting of their imperfections as well as their partners, and more likely to be understanding when there is conflict.

- **Self-compassion and self-esteem are the same:** This is another misconception some people have about self-compassion. They believe it is the same as self-confidence; therefore, they do not need it because they already feel confident in themselves and their abilities. Self-esteem can impact your performance and, ultimately, your results. When things go well, we often feel confident. When things do not go as well as we expected, our self-esteem suffers. While confidence is required to succeed, too much self-confidence can result in an inflated view of yourself, and you may end up making reckless decisions. Self-compassion allows you to be emotionally resilient both in challenging times and during successful ones. It enables you to view situations objectively and encourages you to make rational decisions.

- **Self-compassion is demoralizing:** Some people believe that if they acknowledge their shortcomings, they will stop doing what is necessary to achieve their goals. Through her studies on self-control and grit, psychologist Angela Duckworth found that the key to success is passion and determination (Fessle, 2018). What separates successful people from those who struggle is holding steadfast to a goal until it is accomplished. Practicing self-compassion allows you to be realistic about where you are now and what it would take for you to achieve your goals. It allows you to acknowledge your limitations but not demotivate you from pursuing your goals.

Developing and Demonstrating Self-Compassion

For some people, self-compassion comes naturally, while for others, it takes time to nurture and develop the skill. Fortunately, like any other skill, you can learn how to be self-compassionate with practice. Though it may look different for everyone, each day gives us plenty of opportunities to practice self-compassion. To effectively practice self-compassion, you must be mindful and present, especially when you are going through challenges.

Here are a few ways you can practice self-compassion, even more when you are going through a difficult time.

- **Treat yourself as you would treat a friend:** Be mindful that you are going through a challenging time in your life. Remember that you are not alone in this struggle and that this is part of the human experience. Be gentle with yourself and talk to yourself positively. For example, rather than say, " I'm so dumb, I should have kept my mouth shut," say, "I'm smart, and my views and opinions matter, though they may differ from those of other people."

- **Become more self-aware:** Talk to yourself like you would to a young child or good friend when you make a mistake. Notice your negative thoughts and reframe them into more loving, positive ones. For example, if you fail at performing a task, instead of saying, " I'm not good at this," say, "I will get better with practice."

- **Regain perspective:** Gain a fresh perspective on the situation or problem you may be facing. This involves taking a step back and viewing your situation in the picture bigger rather than focusing on the current negative aspects. Regaining perspective can help you gain a new outlook on life—instead of seeing challenges as obstacles, you look for opportunities to learn and creative ideas to solve the problem.

- **Check-in with yourself throughout the day:** Ask yourself, "What do I need right now?" Perhaps the reason you feel cranky is because you need some rest. Maybe you need to take an hour's break to recharge yourself. Self-care involves listening to and then addressing your needs. Are you feeling less energetic and uninspired? Try changing your diet, exercising more, staying hydrated, and getting enough sleep. Are you feeling upset? Check your environment—who or what could be causing these feelings. Be mindful of your surroundings and identify the things that affect you emotionally.

- **Find small ways to practice self-kindness in difficult moments:** Being kind to yourself may seem like a foreign concept at first if you are not used to it. We often find it is easier to care for and understand other people's shortcomings than our own. Remember, self-compassion involves noticing when you are struggling and recognizing that your experience is part of being human. So, be kind to yourself rather than beat yourself up for your mistakes; embrace them, love yourself, and know that your identity is not defined by your outcomes—you are more than that.

Compassion starts with you. Without taking care of your needs and caring for yourself, it will be difficult to extend kindness, empathy, and understanding toward others.

All these elements of compassion weave together in the process of developing a positive mindset. When you take better care of yourself during adverse times, you cultivate a positive outlook on life.

There is so much good that surrounds us. It takes changing your perspective to realize how blessed you are and that you are not a victim in this life but that you have gifts and talents you can use to initiate the changes you desire in your life.

You are halfway through "Grow Your Positive Mindset."

By sharing your thoughts about this book on Amazon, you are not just writing a review. You are lighting the way for others to develop their positive mindset. Your opinion matters to us, and we kindly request a few moments of your time to leave a review.

To leave a review on Amazon:

* Grab your device: open the Amazon app
* Open your camera app
* Point your mobile device at the QR code below
* The review page will appear in your web browser

Your review means the world to us. It's like passing on a secret map to treasure. This book comes to life when you share what you have learned.

You are playing a big part in keeping this circle of learning alive. Your voice matters. By leaving your review, you are helping countless others like you who are eager to transform their lives.

Thank you!

Chapter 7

Seeing the Bright Side:
Shaping a Positive Outlook by
Recognizing Goodness

Be the change that you wish to see in the world.
–Mahatma Gandhi

At the beginning of Chapter 4, I asked the question: "Have you been searching for the secret to happiness?" We are all searching for some form of meaning and purpose in life, but what does it mean to truly be happy? Does it mean we have to be free of challenges?

There are numerous concepts and ideas on what true happiness means and how you can cultivate it. The objective of most mindfulness practices is to achieve enduring happiness, with an emphasis on being grateful and content with your circumstances.

Another concept of happiness suggests that to be happy, we must live in alignment with our values, ensuring that our basic needs are met.

In a world of challenges and uncertainties, maintaining a positive outlook despite the challenges we face can be life changing. This is not denying the reality, but it is more about finding the silver lining in every situation and remaining optimistic through life's turbulence.

You can experience plenty of benefits when you maintain a positive attitude in every situation. From improved mental and emotional well-being to improved problem-solving skills and building stronger bonds in your relationships, optimism can help you reframe your thoughts about life in general.

There is no doubt that when you are in the face of adversity, it can be difficult to remain optimistic. For example, when you lose someone close to you or the job that pays the bills, often such a situation can leave you feeling like the world just came crashing down in front of you. You may not know how you will make it through another day but by remaining optimistic, you train your mind to see possibilities rather than limitations in every situation. This can help you cultivate a sense of gratitude and satisfaction.

When you practice gratitude daily, you raise your awareness and can identify more blessings to be grateful for. Simply put, you program your mind to see the good around you while embracing your current circumstances. This can improve your problem-solving skills. Rather than being stuck in pessimistic thinking, an optimistic mindset encourages creativity and finding solutions to your challenges. When you stay hopeful despite unfavorable circumstances, you develop adaptability and resourcefulness. Rather than feel defeated, you look for the silver lining in your situation.

Embrace Forgiveness and Acceptance

Feeling betrayed can be an incredibly difficult experience. It hurts to be wronged by the people—especially those you love. But is it possible to forgive the people who have wronged us? And is forgiving someone not condoning their behavior? Forgiveness is, in essence, letting go of feelings of anger, resentment, and lingering emotions toward someone who wronged you. Forgiving the people who have hurt you can prove to be a difficult task. However, as difficult as it may be, it is the best thing you can do for yourself and those around you. It is just as much a gift to yourself as it is to them.

To forgive means to cease to feel resentment against an offender or to give up resentment of or claim to requital (*Definition of Forgive,* 2019). It is an inner state of mind, and it is dependent on no one but you. Your ability to forgive someone often has very little to do with the person who hurt you or what they did but everything to do with you. Are you willing to make a mental shift and change how you feel and act toward the person? Just because you forgive someone does not mean you accept their behavior. It just means you have made peace with what happened and are ready to move on with your life.

It is natural to feel reluctant to forgive. It is a way we protect ourselves—the fight or flight response, which is part of the human instinct. When our security is threatened, we tend to want to strike back or punish those who have wronged us (Regan, 2022).

Perhaps you want to forgive someone, but you are not sure where to begin.

There are different ways you can practice forgiveness, and we will delve deeper into why you should choose to forgive and not harbor resentment in Chapter 10.

The Difference Between Forgiveness and Acceptance

Is forgiveness and acceptance the same? Both terms are key to our mental, emotional, and physical health; however, they have notable differences, and it is important to understand these differences when deciding whether or not to forgive.

Sometimes, people can say or behave in ways that hurt us, and we have no control over the situation. Take children, for instance: When we were young, we were vulnerable to the adults around us. We had no say, power, or control over an adult's anger or frustration. As adults, we still have the same vulnerability and feel hurt when we are offended. The difference is that we just learn to cover it up and not walk around crying or screaming when we are upset like children do when they are upset.

Unforgiveness has negative consequences on your overall health and well-being. Choosing to hold a grudge creates a negative emotional and mental state of mind. It can impact the way you live your life, your life experiences, and the type of people you attract in your life.

Forgiveness is a choice you make so you can heal and move on with your life. Without forgiveness and healing, it is difficult to practice self-love and self-acceptance. You end up bitter, resentful, and pessimistic about life and miss so out on the wonderful experiences life has to offer. But forgiveness does not mean acceptance. It does not mean you are okay with being ill-treated or that you overlook what someone did to you. You forgive people so you can free yourself from negative emotions such as anger, resentment, and strife that may be clouding your life.

If you do not forgive, you end up being the one walking carrying all the burden—that is, anger and sadness, while the person who hurt you lives their life.

Acceptance, on the other hand, is more about acknowledging what happened and understanding that you cannot change what happened in the past. All you can do is embrace the situation and draw lessons from it. While it can be challenging to learn from negative experiences, there is always something that comes out of it that you can be grateful for.

To embrace forgiveness,

- **Understand why forgiving is important:** Before you begin to forgive, understand why you want to. Do you want to forgive the other person and heal the relationship? Or do you want to let go of the anger? Identifying your reasons for practicing forgiveness can help you realize the value of releasing emotional baggage and how healing can lay the foundation for better communication in your relationships.

- **Assess who or what needs to be forgiven:** From this place of understanding, begin to think about the situation and person in question. This is when you will decide whether or not you can forgive the other person. Have they shown remorse for their action, such that you want to see past their actions? Have they apologized for what they did and earned back your trust? Have they explained that it was not their intention to hurt you? And do you believe them? This is a crucial step in the process of forgiving. It lays the foundation for how you will proceed with the relationship. Remember, one key aspect of forgiveness is safety. Do you feel safe—physically and emotionally around this person? When you separate someone's actions from who they are, you can ease into forgiveness.

- **Do some inner work:** Forgiveness requires doing the inner work. When you feel hurt by the actions of others, sometimes it is because of your triggers—it is instinctual if you have been in the past. Ask yourself if you are holding onto anger out of fear or a grudge. And how is that energy affecting your life? As painful as your life experiences may be, recognizing that forgiveness is a gift to yourself can help you heal and grow.

- **Choose to release and forgive:** Once you have done the inner work, you can choose to let go and forgive. Remember, forgiveness is a choice, and you do not necessarily have to say, "I forgive you," to the person. You could write it on a piece of paper and let it go. This has a similar effect as telling the individual that you forgive them. Alternatively, you can tell the person that you are choosing to let it go. It is possible to forgive someone and at the same time say, "You treated me unfairly, and you hurt me—and that is unacceptable behavior, but I'm choosing to forgive you. I'm choosing to let it go so I can move forward.

Work Toward a Minimalist Lifestyle

While the meaning of minimalism differs from person to person, a minimalistic lifestyle involves intentionally focusing on what is important in your life. For some people, this means getting rid of the stuff they do not need that does not add value and bring joy to their lives—this includes objects and people.

How do you create a minimalistic lifestyle? Well, first, you must identify what is essential in your life and be willing to let go of the rest. When you remove the stuff you do not need, you free up your time and space to focus on the things that are meaningful to you.

Scientific research suggests that clutter can increase cortisol levels and disrupt focus (Smak, 2017). Prolonged exposure to high cortisol levels can be detrimental to mental and physical well-being. Imagine waking up each morning in a cluttered bedroom, with clothes all over the floor and surfaces. As you prepare for work, you bump into stuff, and the clutter gets in the way of starting your day in a relaxed and calm environment, triggering a stress response and panic, which results in the rest of the day turning chaotic. Being exposed to clutter every day can disrupt your ability to be calm, relaxed, and focused. This ultimately impacts your quality of life.

More is what society encourages—more cars, more clothes, shoes, accessories, furniture, and so on. The constant desire to have more is often associated with social status, control, security, and comfort. But the more you desire to fill your world with material stuff, the further you drift away from the things that truly matter and have meaning. This is not to say you should not reward yourself from time to time for your hard work, but be conscious of what is important to you and adds value to your well-being.

The easiest way to start living a minimalist lifestyle is to:

- **Assess the people around you:** Surround yourself with people who encourage, support, challenge, love, and bring you joy. Ask yourself if the people in your social circle add value to your life. Cutting ties with people can be complicated, especially with family members for example, if you have a toxic family member, it may be tough to separate yourself from them. This is why setting boundaries is crucial. Boundaries draw the line and teach people how to treat you. Detaching from people requires you to learn to be physically present but not allow other people's actions to trigger your emotions. Try to avoid all attempts to engage in conflicts or arguments.

- **Assess the stuff that surrounds you:** When it comes to material stuff, ask yourself if you need it, use it often, and if it is helping you in any way. If you have no use for the item, you are probably better off without it.

- **Start small:** If you are not sure whether or not you should keep an item or get rid of it, make a list of pros and cons. Decluttering often gets easier with time.

- **Simplify your schedule:** Avoid stretching yourself beyond your limits and overcommitting work that can easily be avoided by saying no. Agree to commit to a task only if you truly want to or are obligated to do so, and remember to prioritize your well-being.

Let Go of Comparison

A lot of factors can cause you to compare yourself with others. These include other people's success. For example, if you are dissatisfied with your appearance, you might start comparing yourself with celebrities and influencers on social media platforms or a new friend who joins your social circle.

Then the comparison begins, and you start to think: "She has everything I do not have," or "He's bright, funny, and everyone loves him. I wish I was as outgoing as he is."

When you compare yourself to someone else, it is like standing in front of the mirror, but all you can see are your imperfections staring right back at you. You start to feel like all your accomplishments are tainted by someone else's achievements. You then start to feel inferior—like you do not measure up, despite your efforts. This pattern often spirals into a depressive mood and can eventually crush you deep down inside.

You can have an excellent intellect, but as long as you feel like someone else is better than you, it will be difficult to experience pleasantness and positivity in your life. Understand this: There may be people who are smarter than you or have more money than you, and others may have accomplished what you want to accomplish, but this does not make you a failure. There are things you excel in and you have excellent personality traits that you probably do not realize when you are focused on comparing your life to that of other people.

When you compare yourself, everything seems less. You might feel like you have fewer friends, you are not pretty enough, or as fun as some of your friends are. You might feel less talented or not as appealing to others. It is these feelings that take away your self-confidence and make you feel like you are worthless. All these feelings and emotions arise because of comparison.

If you want to stop comparing yourself to others,

- **Identify your inner critic when it takes over:** An awareness of your inner critic gives it less power over you and allows you to shift your thoughts from comparison. Instead of comparing yourself to others, you develop self-compassion and accept your current circumstances.

- **Be your best friend:** You may be considered a good friend by your social circle, but are you a good friend to yourself? If a friend was going through a crisis, how would you comfort them? You are likely to sit with them and talk about their feelings rather than say things like, "What were you thinking," or "You're stupid." You would comfort and remind them that they are a wonderful person. You would hug them and reassure them that everything will be okay. Speak to yourself with love and understanding, as you would to a friend you care about. Encourage and remind yourself of all the reasons you are amazing and talented. If you cannot say something negative to a friend, then do not say it to yourself.

- **Keep a record of your achievements:** When you compare yourself to others, your focus is more on their abilities and achievements, and in the process, you forget your own. So, keep a record of your achievements, no matter how small. If you succeed at a work project, record it. If you managed to go to the gym despite the lack of motivation to do so, write it down. Looking at all your accomplishments can increase your self-esteem. You gain a sense of pride knowing that you achieved your goal.

- **Practice self-care and self-love:** Self-care not only involves grooming yourself, but it also requires honest and continuous introspection. It is a process of looking inward and working on some of the emotional issues you may be facing. Sometimes, comparison can be a result of your past experiences. For example, if you were judged or criticized a lot growing up, you may feel insecure as an adult if you have not worked through your emotions. To overcome comparison, keep a journal and write down your thoughts, particularly when you start comparing yourself to someone else. Observe your thoughts and decide whether or not they are true or if they are a result of feeling insecure and inadequate.

- **Be proactive:** When you decide to stop comparing yourself to others, you get clearer on your unique skills, talents, and abilities, gain more confidence in yourself, and no longer see other people's success as a threat to yours. You stop feeling overburdened by feelings of inadequacy, worry, envy, and jealousy and start celebrating the success of others, as well as your own.

Shaking off comparison allows you to enjoy life again and focus on what you want to accomplish and how you can go about it.

Help Yourself by Helping Others

You may have helped someone in the past by giving them your time, attention, and money, or solving a problem for them. You know when someone shows their sincere appreciation and gratitude, you are met with a warm feeling that matches nothing else in this world.

The satisfaction you feel after genuinely helping someone and knowing that your effort means so much to them can help you find purpose and meaning in life.

Helping other people is key to life satisfaction. Helping others does not only have a positive impact on the people you are helping, but it is good for your well-being as well. The results of a study carried out in 2015 on 77 participants show that helping others can reduce stress levels. The participants were asked about stressful events that take place daily, such as their work duties, commute, responsibilities at home, and finances. They were also asked to keep track of the behaviors that helped them cope—any small acts of kindness they did and the emotions linked to these behaviors (Scott, 2019).

Researchers found that participants who performed more acts of kindness each day experienced less stress. On days when they did not perform any acts of kindness, participants reported worse moods and poor mental health.

When we feel stressed, we often turn to others for social support, but results from recent studies suggest that proactively performing acts of kindness can be an effective strategy for coping with everyday stress.

To live a happier and more fulfilling life, you should develop a desire to help others because that, in turn, has benefits for you.

Here are a few more reasons why you should help others.

- **It can boost your mood:** We all want to gain a sense of meaning in life, and making a positive difference in the world can increase your happiness. One study showed that helping others through volunteer work can enhance happiness (*10 Keys to Happier Living*, n.d.) By helping others and being appreciated for your efforts, your body releases endorphins, which improve your mood and boost self-esteem.

- **It builds stronger relationship bonds:** Helping others is a two-way street where you do something good for someone, and you receive the same kind of treatment. When you positively impact someone's life, you feel connected to them. Through cooperation, you both build trust, which strengthens your bond. When you help others, you reinforce your social connections.

- **It builds resilience:** While most people may feel like helping others adds more stress to their lives, sometimes it doesn't; instead, it can help you manage stress better. By looking at other people's challenges, you can take that point of view into your own. This builds acceptance and understanding that hardships are a part of the human experience. Instead of taking things personally, you become more resilient and push through difficult situations.

- **It is good for your career:** There are many factors to consider when searching for the right career. Creative freedom, meaning, and autonomy are key factors to consider. However, one of the biggest factors to consider is how your work impacts others. People who choose to pursue careers in the medical profession, religious set-ups, or firefighting services often rate the highest job satisfaction. The link between these professions is they all help people daily.

With so many distractions surrounding us every day, it can be challenging to create time and space to enjoy life's simple pleasures, such as spending quality time with loved ones, getting creative, exercising, or setting aside time for relaxation. Physical, digital, and mental clutter consumes our time and focus, resulting in high levels of stress and anxiety and an overwhelming sense of dissatisfaction. To live a more fulfilling life, consider decluttering your life and eliminating everything that does not add value to your life—including relationships that no longer serve you.

Life does not always deal us the right cards but comparing your life to someone else's can deprive you of the joy of living and make you feel more miserable. It can lead to self-doubt, and you end up finding it difficult to pursue your goals because you do not feel good enough or talented enough. The truth is, there will always be someone more talented, intelligent, smart, or outgoing than you. There will always be someone with more money, material possessions, and a higher social status than you; however, no one is like you. Knowing your value can help you unapologetically express your individuality and reach your full potential. It changes your perspective on life and how you view yourself—and it all starts with reprogramming your thought processes and cultivating optimism.

Chapter 8

MASTERING OPTIMISM: STRATEGIES TO REWIRE YOUR THOUGHT PATTERNS

We cannot direct the wind, but we can adjust the sails. –Dolly Parton

Are you the type of person who always sees the glass as half-full or half-empty? Well, if you always find it difficult to see the positives in your everyday life, a negative attitude could be getting in the way of achieving your goals.

Pessimism can be detrimental to your mental health and impacts the decisions you make about your future. While adopting a positive outlook is often easier said than done, it is an effective way to cultivate gratitude and develop the motivation you need to keep working toward your dreams, even when you face setbacks.

Now, take a moment to reflect on some of the events that took place today. You can grab a pen and your journal and write down the specifics of each event.

So, what was the outcome? Did you have more positive experiences than negative ones? Was it something positive:

121

"My day's going great! I went to work, and my project pitch was a success. The client loved it! Then, my colleagues and I went out for a late lunch to celebrate our victory." Or did your mind bring up all the stuff that went wrong: "I was late for work because I spent the entire night preparing for my presentation and did not get enough sleep. Then I had to sit in traffic for over 30 minutes, only to get to work and have my boss on my neck, about why I was late. I hate my job!"

What Is Optimism?

Optimism is a state of mind. It is a mental attitude that involves being hopeful and confident in your success and the future despite your present circumstances. An optimistic attitude can be a result of different factors like genetics, upbringing, culture, and other environmental influences. Research suggests that genetics account for around 25% of optimism in us. The results of another study show that age is a key determinant of optimism, and that optimism increases through young adulthood, up to between the ages 55 and 70, and then declines in older adulthood (Scott, n.d.)

When you are optimistic, you view tough times as learning experiences or temporary setbacks. Your worst day can be the foundation of a better tomorrow.

Optimism vs. Pessimism

While optimism is remaining hopeful for better future circumstances, pessimism, on the other hand, is a negative mental attitude that tends to emphasize negative aspects, conditions, and possibilities or to expect the worst possible outcome *(Definition of Pessimism, n.d.)*

Optimism allows you to see the positive side of every situation. You become expectant of things turning out well because you trust in your skills and abilities to solve problems. Pessimism makes you focus on everything that is going wrong, and you end up expecting poor results from your performance.

We all experience times when we are less optimistic, often when we are going through challenging times. But the good news is that if you tend to be more pessimistic than optimistic about your future, you are not destined to always have this mindset. You can adjust the way you view life and develop a more positive outlook.

Why Is Optimism Important?

Life is unpredictable. You can never tell what could happen the next hour, day, week, or year. When something unexpected happens, it can be nerve-wracking and throw you off balance. This often triggers negative emotions. One way to overcome these negative emotions is to maintain a positive attitude.

Optimism is a mental attitude that sees new things as opportunities, transitions as improvements, pitfalls as setbacks, and challenges as learning experiences.

To help you cultivate a positive attitude, here are some key benefits of optimism and why it is an important skill to learn.

Optimism Promotes a Healthier Lifestyle

Research shows that thinking positively can help us live happier, more successful, and healthier lives (*Why Is*

Optimism Important? (26 Benefits of Optimism), 2022). Maintaining a positive outlook can alleviate stress and other mental health disorders. Instead of focusing on your struggles, you focus on the good that surrounds you. Even in the darkest of situations, there is always a silver lining. It may not come in the form of solving your situation; however, the lessons you learn from setbacks are priceless. The best thing is that you can choose and learn to be optimistic—even if you may have a pessimistic attitude.

Optimism Improves Memory and Cognitive Functions

Optimism can improve your memory. When you recall positive memories, you improve your memory and brain processes. This makes it easier for you to remember positive past events because of the emotions associated with them. It also enables you to engage in behaviors that keep your brain healthy. For example, if you think positively about the future, you are likely to develop healthy habits such as eating healthily and exercising regularly.

Positivity can also improve your focus and attention. When you maintain a positive outlook, you are more likely to focus on the things that have value and meaning to you and less likely to be distracted by things that do not serve you. This promotes learning and creativity. Why is this so? It is partly because an optimistic mindset stretches your mental capacity and inspires you to challenge yourself mentally and intellectually. This, in turn, strengthens your mind and keeps your mind sharp.

Optimism Builds Resilience

Staying optimistic in the face of challenges builds resilience and enables you to cope better in difficult life circumstances. When something tragic happens, it becomes easier for you to pick yourself up and keep moving. It also means that when you experience good in your life, you can keep pursuing your goals instead of getting stuck in procrastination and self-doubt for too long.

An optimistic attitude allows you to:

- build resilience in the face of challenges because you do not see problems as permanent but as learning experiences. Maintaining a positive outlook can help you focus on your strengths rather than your weaknesses. You develop the ability to look for solutions rather than dwelling on problems, which can improve your problem-solving skills.

- develop more confidence. When things go wrong, rather than feel helpless and defeated, you look for effective solutions to deal with problems.

- be energetic and act quickly when you face a setback, for example, losing a job or business. You can start looking for alternative ways to earn income rather than wallow in self-pity.

- live a healthier lifestyle. Because optimism builds confidence in your future, you may develop healthy eating habits, exercise more, and go for regular health checkups so you can stay healthy.

- build a supportive social network and social support. You need people around you who will uplift and inspire, even when you go through tough times.

- develop a growth mindset. A positive outlook enables you to see challenges as opportunities to expand your knowledge rather than view them as threats to your self-worth. This can inspire you to stay committed to your goals even when you do not get the results you had hoped for.

Promotes Better Physical Health

When you are optimistic, you realize the beauty that is in the world and appreciate the simple pleasures of life, like taking a walk in the park or walking barefoot on the soft grass, which makes it easier to get out and explore the world out there. You will be amazed at how a 30-minute walk in the park can improve your health and your mind.

Optimism enables you to live an active lifestyle. When you truly enjoy your life and are content with it, it is easier to practice self-care. If you believe that exercise is good for your well-being, you will find it much easier to schedule workout sessions each week.

So, if you want to get active, look at the bright side of life and cultivate a positive attitude each day.

Lowers the Risk of Anxiety and Depression

Optimism allows you to deal with challenges objectively, which can lower stress levels and improve your mental health. Managing stress is crucial to your overall well-being. It is not only beneficial for your physical and mental health but can positively impact your relationships as well. Happy people attract other happy people. When you are optimistic, you are more likely to take control of any situation and communicate better with loved ones. This gives you more control over your life and how you live.

Often, when people feel like life is happening to them, it is because they lose control over it. They merely exist instead of creating the life they desire. Optimism involves realizing that your success in life depends on you and no one else. When things go south, you do not blame others for your mishaps, nor do you judge yourself. You simply understand that things did not work out this time, but you will keep trying until you succeed. Rather than dwell on negative thoughts and emotions, you look for ways to improve.

And yes, it is crucial to bear in mind that a positive attitude is not a remedy for everything. There will be times when things do not work according to your plan, no matter how optimistic you are. But if you can train your mind to focus more on the positive than the negative aspects of your life, you will be well on your way to a happier and more fulfilling life.

Optimism Can Improve Productivity and Increase Job Satisfaction

Besides improving your overall health and well-being, a positive outlook on life can have a significant impact on your productivity and job satisfaction. This is partly because it builds resilience and allows you to pursue your goals despite the challenges you may encounter. When you are optimistic, you develop the ability to shrug off setbacks and stay on track rather than be thrown off course. This kind of mental attitude can help you stay on top of your goals and get through adverse times at work and in your personal life. It allows you to come out stronger and more productive.

It Can Help You Recover Quickly from Setbacks

Optimism is a mental attitude that can help you stay positive and hopeful even in the face of challenges. It encourages perseverance and allows you not to give up when you face setbacks. This does not mean you will always be happy. What it means is that you acknowledge your circumstances and develop the ability to bounce back from failure. When things do not pan out the way you planned, you can use your outcomes as a source of motivation to come back stronger than before. For example, if you did not get that promotion, you worked so hard for, look at the brighter side and ask yourself what you did right and where you need to improve. Think of ways you can improve and take the lessons from the experience and use them for your growth. If you work hard enough, perhaps you might land that promotion next year or even get a better position,

This experience can help you prepare for the future. You never know what opportunities will present themselves after failure it is important to stay prepared and never give up.

It Allows You to Have More Fulfilling Experiences

When you are optimistic, you raise your awareness of what is happening in the present moment and do not put much focus on what might happen in the future. When you focus on being present, you feel more grounded and connected, which allows you to experience and enjoy life. Most people are so focused on running errands and chasing goals that they do not pay attention to their needs. Maintaining a positive outlook and living in the moment allows you to not only exist but to live your life.

This allows you to have control over your mind and not have it wander off to negative thoughts from the past or anxiety about the future, and if it wanders off, you can easily snap out of negative thinking and bring yourself back to the present moment again.

When you are present, you become more connected to others. This is because when you are aware of what is happening around you, you listen more closely to what people are saying without any distractions.

How to Become More Optimistic

Becoming mentally fit involves learning how to control your thoughts so you can live a happier, healthier life and feel good about yourself, no matter your circumstances.

Positivity is not about ignoring the stuff that goes wrong in your life or pretending things do not go wrong from time to time, but it is about choosing to focus more on the positive aspects of a situation rather than the negatives.

If you ask any successful person to reveal the secret to success, fulfilling your goals, and being content, they'll probably say that optimism is key.

So, here are a few ideas that can help you develop a positive attitude, overcome challenges, and accomplish your goals.

Notice the Good Things That Happen Around You Daily

Optimism involves self-evaluation. At the end of the day, take a few minutes to go over the events that took place and come up with a list of the positive aspects of your day. It could be that you completed your daily tasks, closed a sale at work, or received a compliment from your boss for your work. Record what went right in your day in your journal. Noticing the good that surrounds you trains your mind to focus on the positive aspects of life rather than focusing on what is going wrong.

Believe That You Can Succeed and Live a Life Filled with Positive Experiences

Develop the habit of speaking positively to yourself and about your life. For example, if you want to succeed in your career, you could say, "If I upskill, I'll have a better chance of landing that promotion." If you want to pass your exams, you could think along the lines of, "If I study, I have a better chance of coming up top in my class," and if you want to build your social circle, you could think along the lines of, "If I volunteer at the local charity, I'll probably meet new people and make new friends."

Create Positive Mantras

What do you want to achieve? Self-confidence, perhaps? Or maybe improve your self-worth? Come up with a daily mantra around the best version of yourself. Affirm it as if you are already the person you envision yourself to be. Your mantra should start with "I am" statements. For example: "I am confident," or "I am worthy of love and respect." Say the mantra out loud every morning when you wake up and in the evening before going to bed.

Saying affirmations or personal mantras in the morning sets the tone for the day and programs your mind to focus more on being the best version of yourself. By repeating these statements daily, they become deeply embedded in your subconscious mind, and you will begin to notice the transformation as you become the person you have been affirming.

Surround Yourself with Optimistic People

When you hang around positive-minded people, their optimism can rub off on you. Spending your time around pessimistic people can keep you trapped in their reality. Like positivity, negativity can rub off on you—leading you to think and act in ways that do not support your future. For example, if you want to succeed in life, being around lazy people will not give you the motivation you need to work toward achieving your goals. Chances are you may slack around and spend time doing things that will not lead to your success. Therefore, it is important to choose the people you spend most of your time with wisely. Check your social circle. Are the people you are giving your time and energy adding value to your life or not?

Find the Good in Challenging Situations

Appreciating the tiny blessings that surround you is the key to developing an optimistic outlook. Celebrating small wins, such as succeeding at a work project after putting in hours of work, can boost your energy levels. Celebrating your wins— even the small ones, can boost your confidence and make you feel good about yourself. Sometimes, when we face a challenging situation, our minds tend to focus more on the problem, but you have the power to shift your thinking and look for something to be grateful for—even if it is something small or the lesson you learned from the challenge that will help you improve your life.

When things don't work out, remember that setbacks are temporary, and the situation will pass. Assess what went wrong, create a strategy, and plan to make a second attempt. For example, if you failed an assessment, ask yourself what you can do to get better results next time. Perhaps you need to set aside more time to study. If you did not get that job you applied for, maybe you need to learn a new skill or polish up on your existing skills, update your resume, and build confidence to answer interview questions.

Reframe Negative Thoughts

When you have a negative thought, stop, and ask yourself, "How can I turn this around into something positive?" For example, if your superior criticized your performance. When you spot thoughts like, "I know my manager doesn't like me. That's why he never appreciates my work," pause a bit and say to yourself, "I have an opportunity to learn and improve my performance. Now, what can I do to produce better results?" This enables you to start asking the right questions such as, "Who can I ask for help?"; "Do I need to put in more hours to achieve better results?" or "Do I have the skills needed to excel in this position?" This allows you to start searching for the answers to how you can equip yourself.

Consciously Think Positive Thoughts

Rather than say, "I'm not good at this," say, "With practice, I can perfect my skills." Learn to think and speak positively. While self-criticism can help you identify areas to work on and inspire you to make changes in your life, it can do more harm than good to your self-esteem and self-belief. Self-criticism can result in low self-esteem and mental health disorders such as anxiety and depression, as well as eating disorders (Shahar, 2017). So, consciously think positive thoughts. And the best part is that you can train your mind to think more positively. One way you can do this is by writing down five things you are grateful for in your life every day. Do this each morning or before you go to bed. If you can identify more than five things you are thankful for it's okay. What's important is that you acknowledge the good that surrounds you.

How to Approach Life with Optimism: Cognitive Restructuring

Positivity can help you deal with unexpected changes, disappointments, and distress. When you maintain a positive attitude, you open yourself to learning from your mistakes instead of feeling defeated.

If you struggle with being optimistic, perhaps you feel like your challenges are insurmountable. The good news is that there are practical steps you can take to help you feel more optimistic.

Practicing cognitive restructuring—a technique that can help you reframe your thoughts and change your beliefs, can help you develop an optimistic attitude toward life. You can enhance positivity in your life and help others cultivate optimism by consciously identifying negative, self-limiting thoughts and replacing them with optimistic ones.

Cognitive Restructuring Techniques

Cognitive restructuring techniques can help you change negative thinking patterns caused by cognitive distortions and mental patterns that are not based on facts or reality.

Cognitive distortions include:

- **Mental filtering:** This involves identifying one negative detail of a situation and focusing more on the emotions and behaviors linked to it.

- **Black-and-white thinking:** This means the inability to identify a middle ground and viewing a situation with a pessimistic attitude.

- **Concluding:** This means jumping to conclusions without sufficient information.

- **Emotional reasoning:** This refers to being aware of your feelings and forming judgments based on these feelings. It involves assuming that something is true because it feels right, though it may not be the case. For example, if you are stuck in an elevator. Anxiety can make you believe that the elevator might suddenly malfunction and plummet down, even though, when you think about it logically, this is not true.

- **Mind-reading:** This is when you assume what others are thinking without proof.

- **Personalization:** often occurs in people with low self-esteem or paranoia. It happens when you assume that what people do or say has to do with you.

- **Labeling:** Occurs when you make general statements about yourself, or others based on the behavior linked to a situation. For example, if you fail at something and automatically believe that you are a failure.

To effectively use this technique, you first need to understand when to use cognitive restructuring. Let us look at some of the steps you can follow:

Assess Your Feelings and Emotions

Cognitive restructuring involves noticing thoughts that bring about negative thoughts and feelings. When practicing cognitive restructuring, take note of when and where your negative thoughts come up. This is because you may be prone to cognitive distortions in certain situations.

Identifying situations that trigger negative thoughts and emotions can help you prepare beforehand. For example, if you have anxiety, you might notice a pattern of magnifying situations. For instance, say you are undergoing an assessment test for a job; your thinking pattern may go something like, "I'm going to fail this assessment and not get this job, and everyone will know that I failed."

Recognizing negative beliefs as they occur is key to cognitive restructuring. That way, you learn to constructively reframe negative ideas and turn them into positive ones. In this case, you could say something like, "I am well prepared for this interview and have the necessary skills needed for the position. If I do not make it, I will assess where I need to improve and apply again next year."

Identify Thoughts That Trigger Emotional Reactions

The first step requires identifying your automatic thoughts that trigger negative emotions. Before restructuring your thinking patterns, you must be aware of your thoughts with no judgment.

We tend to magnify challenges when, in actuality, they are not as insurmountable as we think they are. Using the previous example of a job assessment, when you believe that you are not going to land the job you are interviewing for, the preceding thoughts could be, "I won't be able to pay my bills and take care of my family. And I'm going to lose our home."

The first step to changing this thinking pattern is to be aware of your thoughts and realize each time you start overemphasizing or magnifying a situation. Ask yourself, "Is this true, or am I trying to predict the future?

You can begin to identify your automatic thoughts every day, and you do not have to go through this process alone. If you need help, seek the help of a trained professional and begin to explore your thoughts in therapy. Taking the initiative to identify maladaptive thinking patterns is crucial because you cannot restructure your thinking without an awareness of what you are thinking in the first place.

Identify Situations That Trigger Negative Thoughts and Emotions

When you realize that a thought is negative and unhealthy for you, you can identify why it is problematic in the first place. This can help you understand why you think along those lines and question whether your beliefs are true or not. For example, if you are anxious about an assessment or job interview, instead of thinking, "I'll fail the job interview," you can start telling yourself, "If I prepare myself and gain confidence to answer the interview questions, I have a better chance of getting hired. All I can do is do the best I can to prepare myself, and if I don't get hired, I will continue searching for employment opportunities on job boards and network more so that I can increase my chances of getting hired.

When you decide that your thoughts are unreasonable and not true, the next step is to make a list of the things you can do instead. In the case of the example above, you could list the things you could do while job hunting, like upskilling, sending out resumes to different companies, creating or updating your LinkedIn profile so that human resources personnel can reach out to you with job opportunities, and so on. This allows you to focus on what you can do and inspires you to continue pursuing your goal.

Gather Evidence

Gathering evidence to determine whether what you think is true or not is key to cognitive restructuring. You can do this by recording the events that trigger a negative response in you— this includes the people you spend time with and the activities you engage in. Record how strong your emotional response is and the memories that came up as a result. You can also gather evidence of whether your thoughts, beliefs, and assumptions are true.

Cognitive distortions are often inaccurate, but they can be deeply ingrained in your subconscious mind. Shifting your mindset and replacing pessimistic thoughts requires evidence to prove their rationality. To do this, you can write down the facts that prove that a belief is accurate versus the facts that show that the belief is incorrect. For example, if you tend to personalize other people's actions, you may blame yourself for things that have nothing to do with you. It would help you to look at the evidence that proves that you are not at fault and that other people's actions have nothing to do with you to prevent paranoia.

Focus on The Objective Facts: Replace Automatic Negative Thoughts with Positive Ones

You can also restructure your thinking patterns by questioning your thoughts and assumptions, especially those that negatively impact your life. Here are some questions you may ask yourself.

- Is this thought based on emotion or facts?

- How can I test the validity of this belief?

- How else can I interpret this information?

- What evidence proves that this thought is accurate?

- What evidence proves that this thought is inaccurate?

- What is the worst that could happen? How can I handle the situation?

For example, if you tend to assume the worst possible outcome in a stressful event, question your thoughts. Make a list of all possible outcomes and ask yourself how likely each possible outcome is to happen. This can open you to consider new possibilities that can override the ones you fear.

Optimism Practices

To practice optimism daily, here are a few ideas to get you started:

Assess Your Ideas While Giving Yourself Credit

Make it a habit to recognize your wins. At the end of each day, take a few moments to ask yourself, "What have I done well today?" Practicing this daily reinforces a positive mindset. Recognizing your wins and how your efforts pay off can help you develop self-confidence, which is key to your success.

When something positive happens in your life, pause a bit and analyze your thought process. Are you giving yourself credit for your efforts? Focus on your strengths and take note of what you did right, both directly and indirectly, to achieve the result. For example, if you aced a job interview, don't just think of how awesome it is that you got the job, but also consider how your skills and knowledge played a role in landing you that position.

Consider How Your Natural Gifts and Talents May Benefit Others

You have innate skills that could change people's lives. Sharing your talents with others can positively impact the lives of many people and give you a sense of fulfillment, joy, and purpose.

If you know what your natural talents are, you can use them in different ways to bless others.

To contribute to society and the world at large, consider what you are good at. Talents can range from qualities, such as problem-solving, researching, having a strong work ethic, or caring for others, to actual skills such as painting, pottery, dancing, singing, or playing a musical instrument. They can also be skills you have learned from past experiences, such as organizing charity events, teaching children to read, or working with young people and helping them overcome some of the challenges they face in school and society. You can use these skills to bring change where you are. For example, if you are good at teaching, why not start a platform where you teach kids how to read? If you play the piano, why not offer piano lessons to students from less fortunate communities?

Once you recognize what your talent is, it becomes easier to choose areas where it can serve a more meaningful purpose and benefit others.

Identify Changes in the Current Situation

One way to cultivate positive thinking and position yourself for success is to form the habit of recognizing any form of improvement in your performance, no matter how small. For example, if your goal is to lose 50 pounds, losing a pound may seem like a small thing, but it is still a win, and it is directing you in the direction of achieving your major goal.

Focus on potential future outcomes to stay optimistic and motivated.

Try to Minimize the Negative

What is getting in the way of your success? Are distractions and obstacles constantly getting in the way of accomplishing your goals? Do you have habits that are getting in the way of your productivity? Or are negative people sabotaging your success? One of the key elements to practicing optimism is to make steady progress. This involves eliminating distractions and anything that gets in the way of your success. You develop optimism through successful outcomes rather than through failure.

Find ways to avoid temptations in your life, keep your priorities straight, and discipline yourself to complete any task you set for yourself.

If you have difficulty telling people you are busy, then let their calls go to voicemail. You will call them back when you have time.

When you face a negative situation, ask yourself what circumstances could have contributed to the situation. If, for instance, you performed poorly on an assignment, is it because you were busy the previous week? Did you perhaps not get enough sleep? Did you have all the resources you needed?

When assessing the situation, remember that this is not a reflection of your weaknesses. It means that it is equally important to look at the negative aspects of a situation as it is to focus on the positive side because it can help you change your behavior in the future and take responsibility for your actions—and this is part of the learning process!

Chapter 9

CRAFTING AND ACHIEVING MEANINGFUL GOALS

Setting goals is the first step in turning the invisible into the visible. –Tony Robbins

Have you thought about where you would like to be in five years? Have you set clear objectives and created a strategy on how to go about achieving your objectives? Do you know what steps you need to follow each day, week, month, and year?

These questions may sound a bit overrated because we all know that life is unpredictable, right? But if you want to succeed in life, you need to take time to think about your future and how you want to design it; therefore, you need to set clear and precise goals that will help you build the life you envision. Setting goals gives you control over the direction of your life. Without goals, you lack focus and direction.

Setting goals can also help you assess whether or not you are succeeding. If, for instance, your goal is to make more money, having a million dollars in the bank is proof that you are making progress in achieving your goal. And if your goal is to be charitable, giving your time and resources to a worthy cause is proof that you are making progress toward fulfilling your goal.

While setting goals is key to your success, it is essential to know how to set them. Saying, "I want..." and expecting it to happen is not going to help you accomplish your goals. You need to follow a process that will help you carefully consider what you want to achieve.

In between where you are now and where you would like to be, you must have well-defined steps that transcend the specifics of your goals. This will allow you to set goals that you can accomplish.

What Are Life Goals?

We all have something significant we want to achieve in life. It could be career-based, personal development, or your health and well-being. This all hinges on what you value most in your life.

Life goals are the things we want to achieve in life that are much more meaningful than just what we need to achieve to survive. Unlike daily tasks or short-term objectives, life goals drive our behaviors in the long run.

There is no single definition for life goals, but they can help us ascertain what we want to experience in alignment with our values. Because life goals are personal ambitions, they take different forms based on your values and aspirations. They give you a sense of direction and make you accountable for achieving your dreams and creating the best version of yourself.

Different Types of Goals

- **Short-term goals:** These are goals you can set for more immediate outcomes. The length of time you give yourself to pursue a short-term goal depends on different factors, such as the amount of effort you need to put in and the resources you have to pursue it. Typically, short-term goals are goals you want to reach by the end of the day, the week, or the month. They may also be small, actionable steps you need to take to achieve your long-term goal. Examples of short-term goals include enrolling in a skills-building course, drinking 8 glasses of water per day, reading 2 books per month, and so on.

- **Long-term goals:** These are goals that you can set that may take a longer period to accomplish. They can also take a significant amount of work to achieve. Long-term goals typically take months, years, or even decades to reach. Examples of long-term goals include starting a small business, purchasing a home, or becoming proficient at a skill.

- **Interpersonal goals:** These are goals centered on building social skills and relationships. It could be relationships with acquaintances, professional connections, close friendships, or family members. Interpersonal goals may include spending more time with loved ones, having important conversations, becoming a better listener, and gaining more confidence to communicate.

- **Professional goals:** These are goals that focus on your career. They might include team goals for your workplace or your professional aspirations. Examples of career goals that you can set and pursue include landing a promotion, improving workplace relationships, and excelling at a sales quota.

- **Financial goals:** These are goals that focus on improving your financial situation. They may include personal or professional finances, such as saving for retirement, paying off debt, building an emergency fund, or budgeting to make a purchase.

- **Academic goals:** These are goals that are related to your education and academic career. You can use them at different stages of your academic career, including high school, undergraduate, graduate, and teaching. Academic goals also include earning a degree, winning a scholarship, publishing your work, or specializing in a skill.

What Is Goal Setting?

Goal setting is the process of deciding what you want to achieve at a particular given time. Goals are the aim or the end toward which effort is directed (Merriam-Webster, 2019b), for example, to learn a specialized skill within a specified time limit. They are the level of competence that we wish to achieve that we can use to assess our current performance. The goal-setting process is crucial because it is the bridge between where you are now and where you want to be when you achieve your goal.

American psychologist Edwin A. Locke developed the goal-setting concept. The main purpose of the goal-setting theory is to understand the link between how the process of setting goals impacts work motivation and performance (Debara, 2022). From there, you can better understand how you can become more successful in achieving your goals.

Establishing what is beneficial to your welfare can help you set goals accordingly. Locke suggests that our lives depend on the process of choosing goals to pursue. If you do not set and execute goals, your chances of success are greatly reduced.

Goal setting is a powerful motivator. If you have ever wondered why some people perform better on tasks than others—even with the same knowledge and abilities. It is because those who succeed are likely to be motivated. To achieve your goals, you must be flexible and adjust your goals based on your circumstances. This can significantly impact your performance and allow you to keep working toward fulfilling your objectives despite some of the challenges you may encounter.

The Importance Goal setting

Most people have dreams. They know what brings them joy and fulfillment and what they'd love to achieve, but often have a vague idea of how to go about it. This is where goal setting comes in. Goals give you focus and alleviate procrastination. When you set clear goals, you know what you're supposed to do at any given time, which will bring you closer to achieving your goals.

Below are some of the benefits of setting clear, attainable, and realistic goals.

Setting Goals Shows You What You Should Focus On

Edwin A. Locke's goal-setting theory suggests that our intentions drive our actions (Houston, 2019). Setting goals and focusing your attention on the specifics of your goals leads you to why you want to achieve the goal, how you will achieve it, and what resources, skills, and assistance you need to achieve your aspirations.

Goals give you laser focus and motivate you to stay on track until you have achieved your desired results. And yes, there may be limitations and setbacks along the way to achieving your dreams; however, the process of setting goals can give you a clear picture of what you want to accomplish. The more you focus your attention on the possibility of achieving something significant, the more inspired you will be to keep working on your goals until you reach them.

Goals Provide Feedback on Your Performance

When you are clear about what you want in life, it becomes easier to assess where you are now and lay out the steps you need to follow to get to where you want to be. Goal setting can act as feedback or a way to assess if you are making progress or far from reaching your goals. This allows you to adjust your behavior accordingly to align with what you want to achieve.

Goal setting Can Promote Happiness

Working toward something important to you increases happiness and gives you a sense of fulfillment. When you do not have clear goals in place, it is easy to procrastinate and put off important tasks that could lead to your success for some other time.

Procrastination not only undermines your performance but also takes away the joy and excitement of working toward your dreams.

Research shows that pursuing and achieving meaningful goals plays a key role in our psychological well-being (Stauner, 2023). Your happiness and emotional fulfillment rely on whether or not you are making progress in your life. The results of the same study on the link between personal goals and the psychology of well-being suggest that setting goals with a time limit and having external motivation, self-determination, and the willingness to invest time and effort can lead to changes in our well-being.

Besides the joy that comes with accomplishing something significant, achieving your goals can stir up positive emotions and lead to happier relationships and more engagement in activities that bring you joy.

Setting Goals Encourages You to Utilize Your Strengths

When we are clear about what is important to us, we can tap into our inner strengths, and the passion for what we want to accomplish is stirred up inside of us. While charting a course for yourself is an exciting adventure, using your strengths and determination to get there increases confidence in your abilities. It makes you realize that you have the power to change your circumstances.

Your strengths may include your optimistic thinking, positive feelings, and actions that make you feel energized and more engaged in your life. They are also behaviors that drive you to perform at your best. When you are optimistic, and your actions align with the goals you set, your confidence increases, and there is no telling how far you can go in life.

Setting Personal Goals

If your goal in life is to find meaning and gain a sense of fulfillment, personal goals can help you get there. Or perhaps you feel uninspired by your personal goals; effective goal setting can help you accomplish them. As humans, we are meant to evolve and not stay the same, and this is why self-improvement is key to your mental and emotional well-being.

Personal goals clarify your future. They can help you grow into the person you envision yourself to be. If you are not clear about what path you want to take in life or how to go about fulfilling your dreams, using your personal goals is an effective way to create a personal vision statement. A vision statement can help you establish what your inspirations are and the things that give you meaning and direction in life.

Our personal and professional lives comprise different elements that can make life seem complicated. There are times we may feel like we are exactly where we are meant to be—when we feel content. And then, there are other times when we feel dissatisfied—like we need a fresh start. A personal vision statement can help when you do not understand how the external and internal worlds are linked. It can improve your focus and help you get your priorities straight.

When you have a clear plan and vision for your life, you gain a sense of pride in your ability to improve and accomplish your goals. Setting vague goals that do not have a strategy to execute them can set you up for failure. It will be difficult for you to measure your progress and see whether you are still on the right path. Without clear and precise goals, you may not even know when you have hit the goal. For example, if your goal is to make more money, this is a great objective to aim for and it could improve your financial situation. However, it does not provide specifics such as how much money you want to make, how you will earn, and how long it will take you to achieve your goal.

How to Achieve Your Goals

While setting big goals is key to your success, putting in place small, actionable steps that will help you achieve your bigger goal is equally important. For example, if you want to earn an extra $5,000 per month, you can aim to sell a $250 product or service to 5 customers a week for a total of $1,250 per week.

Success requires you to set SMART goals that will give you a clear road map to achieving your desired outcomes.

How to Set SMART Goals

SMART goal setting lays the groundwork to achieve your personal and professional goals. Your goals must be:

- **Specific:** For example, if you want to save for retirement, instead of setting your goal as "I need to save money," try focusing on how you will do it. Your goal could look something like, "Pay off debt first, so I can start building my retirement savings." Or, "I will use my digital marketing skills to start a digital marketing agency to increase my income." Remember, goals should direct you on the path to achieving your desired results.

- **Measurable:** You should be able to assess your progress and see whether or not you are improving. For example, in the case of our example above, your goal could be to save $10,000 per year toward your retirement savings. Doing this makes it easier to track when you have reached your goal.

- **Attainable:** Will you be able to save $10,000 per year? Do you have enough resources to help you achieve your goal? Setting unrealistic goals can make you lose motivation easily because it is difficult to achieve the goal.

- **Relevant:** They should be aligned with your values, dreams, and aspirations.

- **Time-bound:** They should have a timeline for their attainment. This creates a sense of urgency and allows you to manage your time wisely. Setting a due date for reaching your goal forces you to pace yourself.

Here are a few more ideas to help you set your SMART goals:

- If you are unsure about what direction to take in life, make self-improvement a top priority in your life. There are plenty of resources you can use, like this book, and courses you can take to help you think long and hard about what you value most and want to achieve in your life. And if it takes you time to figure out your purpose, try not to be hard on yourself. Great things take time to accomplish. As George Bernard

Shaw once said, "Life isn't about finding yourself. Life is about creating yourself" (Shah,2022). And you can create yourself as many times as you like as your dreams and aspirations change.

- Ask yourself why you are setting that specific goal. Is it going to help you achieve inner peace and financial stability, or is it just a hobby that sparks creativity in you and brings you fulfillment?

- Set goals based on what you can control. This can motivate you to act on your goals and it gives you a sense of control over your future.

- Frame your goals in a positive tone. For example, Instead of setting a goal like, "Watch less television in the evening," your goal should be something like, "Do a one-hour physical exercise every evening."

- Create an action plan or a to-do list to help you achieve your goals. This gives you a clear direction on what steps to take and your responsibilities in accomplishing your goals.

Write Down Your Goals

The act of writing down your goals makes them tangible and gives you a reference point when you are assessing your progress. When writing your goals, start your statements with "I will" instead of " I would like to," "I want to," or "I might." For example, "I will save 10% of my income every month," instead of saying, "I want to save 10 of my income every month." The first statement is empowering and can help you visualize yourself saving that 10% and achieving your goal.

The second statement lacks passion—it is easy to fall into the trick of giving excuses or getting sidetracked.

Break It Down

Another strategy that could make your goals attainable is the 90-day sprint. Instead of setting one big goal, break it down into smaller tasks that you can complete every day. For example, if your fitness goal is to build muscle, here is an example of how you could plan your 90-day sprint.

Identify Where You Are Now

First, establish where you are in terms of fitness.

- Are you physically fit or weak?

- How flexible are you?

- Do you feel any tension in any part of your body, for instance, your calves?

Establishing a baseline or where you are at the moment determines your current threshold. Threshold refers to the level or point at which the results of what you are working on begin to show.

Try to be realistic about what you can do within 90 days. Is it possible to see your desired results in 90 days? This can help you adjust your goals accordingly.

Define Your Criteria for Success

Next, write down what success means to you. How will you know that you've reached your goal? To feel encouraged and a sense of accomplishment, you want to see positive results within 90 days. Within the first 30 days, you should be able to measure your progress.

If you are trying to build muscle in a specific area of your body, record the measurements of the area you are working on before you begin using a tap measure and record your current measurements every week. With an effective workout and eating plan, you should begin to see tangible results within 30 days or so.

Create a Detailed Plan to Reach Your Goal In 90 Days

The next step is to devise a plan for how you will go about tackling the smaller goals you set every day. Determine what action you would take to achieve your desired results. Remember that writing down your goals only will not yield results. You must take immediate action and stay consistent throughout the 90 days to reach your goals. Build resistance, push through the challenges you may encounter, and lean into the difficulties. Before you know it, you will be way ahead of those who set goals and create a great plan but never dare to follow through until they reach their goals.

Often, we overlook planning the steps we should take to get to the finishing line. Planning the steps that you need to follow on your way to achieving your goal and crossing them out one by one as you complete each step will help you measure your progress. This is crucial if you are setting long-term goals.

90 days is ample time for you to see massive results. Ensure that you stick to your plan, show up every day, be consistent, and you will accomplish what you set out to do.

Focus On the Bigger Picture

Often, we are afraid of setting huge goals because of the fear of failure. While failure may be a harsh reality when pursuing your dreams, understand that failure is part of success. When you change the way you view setbacks and positively frame your thinking processes, you will realize that what we refer to as failure is nothing more than feedback from our outcomes, signaling that we still have certain areas we need to work on. If your past failures or mistakes are diminishing your confidence in your abilities to pursue new goals, there are ways you can motivate yourself and move past your fears.

To achieve this:

- **Celebrate the small wins:** If, for instance, your goal last year was to read 20 books and you managed to read only nine. Rather than be hard on yourself and think that you failed to achieve your objective, remind yourself that this is still progress and proof that you can improve and transform your life. This on its own is an achievement, so celebrate your small wins because they add up with time, and before you know it, you will have accomplished something significant.

- **Think about other benefits related to achieving your goal:** Pursuing a goal is not only about reaching your desired outcome. It is a journey filled with lessons, and if you pay attention, you may even discover new passions along the way. For example, if you set a financial goal, say you want to get out of debt and improve your finances. The lessons you learn along the way on improving personal finance can ignite a passion in you to teach others about personal finance. While your initial goal was to improve your finances, you end up helping others achieve financial freedom too. So, each time you achieve a goal, ask yourself, "What lessons did I learn from trying to reach my goal?"

- **Analyze your performance:** Though dwelling on your failures is not an effective way to deal with setbacks, it is important to trace your steps and understand why your plans did not pan out. Objective analysis is key to success. It can help you better understand where you went wrong and how you can improve your performance. If, for some reason, you feel like you cannot carry out an objective analysis yourself, ask a friend or family member to do a post-failure autopsy. They may be able to provide you with a true analysis of your performance that can help you better understand yourself.

Personal Goals You Can Set for Yourself

Here are four examples of personal goals you can set for yourself.

Financial Goals

Financial goals are related to improving your finances. They can help you get out of debt, stay on top of your budget, or work towards a specific investment plan.

Examples of financial goals include:

- paying off your debt within one year.

- reducing spending by 20%.

- saving a down payment to purchase a home in two years.

- setting aside $25,000 toward your retirement savings each year.

- building an emergency fund in the next 6 months.

Career Goals

Career goals are usually a top priority for most people when they think about the goals they want to set for themselves. Career goals can range from minor responsibilities to larger goals, such as leadership positions and increasing your earnings.

Career goals are objectives that you set to help you progress in your professional life. Like other SMART goals, career goals must have a time frame to motivate you to keep working toward achieving them. For example, if your career goal is to become the CEO of the organization you work for in the next 10 years, you may need to work harder and acquire the necessary skills for that position.

Your professional goals can be short-term or long-term. Understanding the importance of setting career goals can help you adjust your personal goals to reflect your personal and professional growth. Setting career goals allows you to establish milestones that will help you measure your progress.

Achieving your professional goals can bring about a sense of fulfillment and confidence in your abilities that inspires you to progress in your career path.

Here are a few career goals you can set for yourself.

- Learn a new skill.

- Develop a strong professional network.

- Get a promotion.

- Improve job performance.

- Earn a higher salary.

- Receive an award or special recognition for your work.

- Switch careers.

- Increase your productivity.

- Start a business.

- Be an expert consultant in your field.

- Increase your creativity and innovation.

Growth Goals

When you set personal goals for yourself, you are approaching your life with an open mind and a desire to succeed in all areas of your life. Personal growth goals are meant to motivate you to accomplish what you want in life. The process of setting personal growth goals opens you up to try new ways of doing things, plan your success, and take action to improve your life. It also allows you to be accountable for your growth and development.

Goals can help you identify your mistakes, learn from them, and make changes using the lessons you draw from the process of achieving them.

Below are a few examples of personal growth goals you can set for yourself.

- Improve your growth mindset by reading books, taking self-improvement courses, or applying daily positive affirmations.

- Be open-minded to new opportunities.

- Wake up at 5 a.m. every morning.

- Learn something new.

- Create work-life balance.

- Develop good habits.

- Improve your communication skills.

- Develop time management skills.

- Learn healthy ways to cope with stress.

Health goals

Health goals are outcomes you desire for your health. These include physical fitness goals, nutritional goals, and mental health goals. To achieve all other goals you set for yourself, you should be healthy physically, mentally, and emotionally. Your health and well-being are crucial to your success because when your health is compromised, it is difficult to follow through with your goals.

Physical Fitness Goals

Here are a few physical fitness goals you can set for yourself:

- try a new physical activity. It could be going hiking, biking, or dancing.

- take a 30-minute walk every day.

- train for 45 minutes every day, three times a week.

- stretch every day.

Nutritional Goals

Your diet goals could be:

- drink more water.

- eat at least five portions of vegetables every day.

- have breakfast every morning.

- eat at the dining table instead of in front of the television.

Mindful eating—being present while eating or drinking and developing awareness of your physical cues and feelings about food—can help you improve your eating habits. Studies show that when you enjoy your meal, your body absorbs more nutrients (Shermer, 2007). So, make mindful eating a priority in your life; it will change how you perceive food and encourage healthy eating.

Mental Health Goals

Your mental health is as important to your well-being as your physical health and your diet. To function at your optimum, you must be in a healthy state of mind. Mental health goals can include practicing mindfulness and meditation, showing gratitude, and creating time to practice self-care. All of these goals can improve your mental health and help you live a healthier life.

Here are a few more mental health goals you can set for yourself.

- Increase your energy levels.

- Reduce stress.

- Maintain good health.

- Reduce pain and risk of illness.

- Practice self-love and self-compassion.

- Set boundaries.

- Get six to seven hours of sleep each day.

- Spend 10 minutes journaling in the morning when you wake up and in the evening before going to bed.

When setting goals, ensure that they align with your values. Your goals must speak to you personally; otherwise, it will be difficult to achieve them. For instance, knowing that exercise is good for heart health does not always motivate you to exercise every day. You have to establish why health goals are important to your life and how they will benefit you in the long run.

If you want to succeed in life, goal setting can help you get where you want to be. While your vision and purpose give you an idea of what you want to accomplish in life, your goals are what will get you to the finish line.

Whether it is personal goals or career goals you set for yourself, the goal-setting process can give you clarity on how to achieve your goals. The act of setting goals on its own can enhance your self-confidence. While you may face challenges along the way, perseverance, resilience, patience, open-mindedness, and willingness to learn from your mistakes can help you fulfill your goals and live the life you envision for yourself.

Even if you do not reach all of your goals on the first attempt, writing them down can give you a deeper sense of fulfillment and contentment.

Chapter 10

UNBURDEN YOUR SOUL: BREAKING THE CHAINS OF RESENTMENT

You're going to go through tough times—that's life. But I say, "Nothing happens to you; it happens for you." See the positive in the negative events. –Joel Osteen

Have you ever wondered what life would be like if we did not have to deal with some of the challenges we encounter in relationships? Perhaps let me rephrase: How would your life be if you did not have to deal with some of the difficult people? Would you be happier, more fulfilled, and able to articulate yourself?

While developing a positive mindset can enhance your optimism and zest for life, we cannot ignore the fact that life is not always a smooth sailing experience. Being optimistic about life does not mean we should ignore life's unpleasant situations, but it means that we should approach unpleasantness more positively and productively.

165

Sometimes people do or say things that hurt us, and we have no control over it. Whether intentionally or unintentionally, being hurt by someone else—especially those closest to you, can have a lasting impact on you. It stirs up negative emotions such as anger, frustration, sadness, confusion, and distress—and all these emotions can leave you with a deep sense of injustice. If left unresolved, these emotions can fester in your mind—causing you to resent the person who wronged you.

While resenting someone for their ill behavior may seem like the right thing to do to prevent the same experience from happening, it is not the best way to resolve conflicts or to deal with the people who hurt you.

Resentment can make you spiteful toward someone or something that causes you pain—whether it is real or just a perception. This can have a lasting effect on you, and this is why some people get attached to their resentments because they feel deeply wronged. Now, the problem with resentment is that it is something you hold within yourself. Instead of affecting the person who has wronged you, it often affects you more.

But how do we handle the people who hurt us? Should we let them walk free while we remain nursing our wounds? And why is it that even when we know that to heal and move past what someone did, we should forgive them, as well as forgive ourselves, we still find it difficult to practice forgiveness?

Being treated unfairly is a sad part of life; unfortunately, we cannot control how people choose to treat us most of the time—and some people are just unaware of how their actions impact other people. It is natural to be angry and resentful when you are hurt; however, harboring resentment can have long-term effects on you, even after you move past the experience.

Before we get to why it is important to forgive so you can assert whether or not you should forgive your offender, let us first gain a better understanding of what resentment is.

What Is Resentment?

Resentment can be defined as anger and disgruntlement experienced when treated unfairly. When we are resentful, we often experience feelings of annoyance, fear, regret, or shame. Resentment can ignite the desire for revenge, whether it is as a result of a small matter or something significant. When you are processing what someone did to you, it is crucial to remember that sometimes resentment can be a result of inadequate expression of your emotions when you are hurt.

Feelings of resentment can arise from a true, perceived, or misunderstood injustice. For example, a comment from a friend, made unintentionally, could offend you and stir up grudging feelings. You are likely to experience the same feelings of resentment when your employer criticizes you. When you recognize this, it becomes easier for you to take a step back and assess the situation rationally.

Resentment not only applies to individual offenders but to large groups of people: For example, religious persecution and racism—which are often a result of deep-rooted resentment.

When we are wronged, we feel victimized because of shame; we express the grudge in the form of anger rather than express how we feel.

Though resentment can dissipate when you realize that you misinterpreted a situation or when your offender apologizes, the emotions may linger on. You may find yourself holding on to negative feelings, replaying the painful experience over and over in your mind. This can make it difficult to let go of anger or the urge for revenge, and as a result, resentment can impact your mental health.

The Benefits of Forgiving Someone

Whether you have been cut off in traffic, betrayed by a loved one, or belittled by a colleague, we all face different situations that can affect our emotions. Sometimes we find ourselves contemplating whether or not to forgive the people who hurt us to maintain relationships. Now, the challenge is that forgiving someone who has done you wrong is easier said than done, which is why sometimes we hold onto that painful experience and choose resentment over forgiveness. However, if you choose to forgive the people who hurt you, there are so many benefits in learning to forgive than holding a grudge—even more for you than the person you are forgiving.

It is crucial to understand that forgiving someone does not mean condoning their actions and forgetting what they did. What it simply means is that you are willing to let go of anger and resentment and any other negative feelings and emotions you have toward the person so you can move forward with your life. This gives you so much power and control over your life because you no longer have to carry the burden of these negative emotions.

Letting go of bitterness can make way for improved mental, emotional, and physical health. It can also lead to healthier relationships and improved self-esteem.

The Harmful Side Effects of Holding Grudges

Bitterness is not good for your overall well-being. It keeps you trapped in anger and makes you dwell on the past rather than move forward with your life.

While you may think that resenting the person you at mad at hurts them, ultimately it affects you instead. Bitterness prevents you from dealing with your emotions and resolving issues. It keeps you trapped in an unpleasant situation or interaction and continues to cause you distress long after the event has passed. Bitterness does not solve the problem or make you feel any better. Studies show that focusing on negative emotions rather than resolving them can be harmful to our well-being (Vanbuskirk, 2021).

Mental Health Effects

Resentment can negatively impact your mental health in different ways. When you are unable to let go of anger, you can feel angrier. Instead of finding an amicable way to resolve the issue and moving on from a negative experience, holding on can keep you enraged—feeling hopeless and bitter. In other words, unforgiveness exposes you to more unpleasant thoughts and emotions, which can encourage negative thinking and a pessimistic attitude. This can cause you to relive the painful experience.

Reliving the negative experience over and over can be emotionally and physically draining and frustrating. It does not resolve the issue but instead enhances your negative emotions. Research shows that focusing on negative emotional events makes it feel like the event happened recently, even when it is not a recent incident (Siedlecka et al. 2015).

Physical Health Effects

Unforgiveness can have profound negative effects on your physical health. This is likely because of the stress that comes with holding a grudge. Chronic stress can impact your cardiovascular health and reproductive, digestive, and immune systems.

Headaches, asthma, insomnia, and upset stomachs can also be a result of high levels of stress. To mitigate stress symptoms, you should find effective ways to release anger and frustration and let go of grudges.

Social Effects

Bitterness not only affects your mental and physical health, but it can also adversely impact your relationships as well. Holding grudges can cause people to be hostile to you, it can ruin your friendships, and limit the number of people in your social circle.

While it is important to forgive the people who hurt you, it is equally important to be aware of the people you spend most of your time with. There are times when it is necessary to end certain relationships or minimize your interaction with certain people—particularly those who are toxic to your well-being.

When you hold grudges, you.

- bring anger into your relationships.

- become caught up in the wrong that you cannot see the good that is in the present moment.

- become anxious, irritable, and depressed.

- become unaligned with your spiritual beliefs.

- lose out on building meaningful relationships with others.

Forgiving and Letting Go of Emotional Burdens

Now, who has never been hurt by other people's words and actions? Whether it is a parent who constantly criticized you when you were young, an employer who has never valued your contribution to the company, or a partner who had an affair. Or, maybe you have gone through a traumatic experience where someone you trust betrayed or abused you physically or emotionally. These wounds can have a lasting impact on you. If left unresolved, they can build up over time and result in bitterness, anger, hatred, and resentment toward the person who hurt you.

While it is understandable to be angry at the person who hurt you, bear in mind that when you hold on to pain, you may be the one who pays the price more than the person who hurt you. Forgiveness can be a difficult thing to do, especially when the person you are forgiving does not feel any remorse about their actions. Forgiving them can feel like you condone their behavior, but that is not the case. When you learn to forgive people, you free yourself mentally and emotionally, and their actions no longer trap you.

Realize that you cannot control other people's actions and understand that the only thing you can control is how you react to certain situations. This gives you back your power and allows you to forgive without holding back.

Learning to Forgive

There are two sides to forgiveness—emotional and decisional. With emotional forgiveness, you allow yourself to move away from negative feelings and no longer dwell on painful experiences. Decisional forgiveness, on the other hand, involves choosing to replace hatred with kindness. When you embrace forgiveness, you also embrace peace, love, and hope. This can usher you on the path of physical, emotional, and spiritual well-being.

There are different ways to go about forgiving someone who has hurt you.

To forgive,

- **Recall and reflect:** Recall the event, your feelings, emotions, as well as your reactions. How has pain and bitterness impacted you? When you realize how anger negatively impacts your life, you can finally lean toward forgiveness and release all the negative emotions associated with the event and the person.

- **Empathize with the person:** Empathy involves understanding the other person's perspective and their emotional experiences. Try to understand the other person's perspective regarding why they hurt you without minimizing the wrong they did. You just might realize that it was not personal but because of what the person was going through. People who hurt others are sometimes themselves hurting and living in a state of fear, anxiety, and pain. Practicing empathy allows you to see your offender as a human being. It broadens your perspective and enables you to slowly release anger and forgive yourself and others.

- **Make a conscious decision to forgive:** When you forgive from a place of understanding, you realize that no one is perfect, as much as you have your imperfections. This allows you to move forward even if that person never apologized, and sometimes, even consider the possibility of rebuilding the relationship.

- **Let go of expectations:** An apology may not always provide comfort or closure. It may not shift your affiliation with the person. Therefore, if you do not have expectations of what the other person should do, you are less likely to be disappointed.

- **Be compassionate:** Address your own shortcomings. Think of a time when you wronged someone, and they forgave you. How did you feel? Recognizing this helps you realize that forgiveness and compassion are altruistic gifts you can offer others. Forgive others to the same extent you would want to be forgiven.

- **Forgive yourself:** Cultivating self-forgiveness can be a difficult thing to do, especially if you have not been practicing self-love and self-acceptance. Learning to be kind to yourself is a skill you can cultivate over time. It requires practice and awareness. Remember that your mistakes are as much a part of your human nature as your strengths.

Does Forgiveness Guarantee Reconciliation?

When deciding to forgive someone, it is important to understand that forgiveness and reconciliation are two completely separate processes. Because they are often lumped together, most people tend to confuse them and think that because they forgave the person, they can salvage the relationship. Unfortunately, combining forgiveness and reconciliation with the belief that reconciling is part of the forgiveness process can lead to excruciating pain and disappointment.

If the painful experience involved someone close to you and you value the relationship, forgiving them may lead to reconciliation; however, it is not always the case. It is also crucial to understand that forgiveness does not require anything from the offender but has everything to do with you choosing to let go of emotional pain. When you realize this, it becomes easier to forgive, even when the person does not offer an apology. For example, you can forgive someone and not reconcile with them. Reconciliation might not be possible if the offender has died or they are not willing to communicate with you, but forgiveness is still possible—even when reconciliation isn't.

Should You Forgive Someone Who Is Not Willing to Change?

Forgiveness is about identifying what you can control in any given situation, and that is your reaction to the event. Getting another person to change is not the point of forgiveness. Take forgiveness as a way to bring you peace, happiness, and emotional and spiritual healing. It is a way you take back your power and not allow the other person or the painful experience to have a hold over you.

Letting Go of Resentment

Holding onto resentment often gives a false sense of power and control over the person or situation. You may think you are protecting yourself from getting hurt again or feel like you are maintaining a psychological advantage. For example, if your partner cheats on you, holding onto resentment can be a defense mechanism to prevent you from getting hurt or pursuing a new relationship. While this may seem like a preventive mechanism, it can take away the joy of living and experiencing meaningful relationships.

At a deeper level, resentment can have a significant impact on your life. The best way to find resolve and inner peace and grow from the experience is to embrace vulnerability. Vulnerability means that you are open about your feelings, needs, and fears rather than hiding them.

When you look at yourself and your relationships with openness, you can appreciate the vulnerabilities that come with being human. Sometimes, we must dig a little deeper to better understand why we must forgive. In the process of diving deep within ourselves, we can see that the human experience is more than what meets the eye—that we are one—we share the same experiences, and people hurt us as much as we have hurt others.

Accept What Happened

Trying to control external circumstances—be it the weather or other people's actions, is a sure way to experience frustration. When you accept that you cannot control everything that happens to you, you can realize that there are other things you can control, such as how you react to the situation, and move on.

While you cannot control the weather, you can still grab an umbrella to protect yourself when it rains. The same applies when you are dealing with people. You cannot control other people's actions, but you can control your reactions and be open about your feelings and expectations.

When someone wrongs you, try to accept that it happened and that there is nothing you can do to change the past, but you can do something different going forward. And keep in mind that accepting a painful experience does not mean that you agree with what happened. What it simply means is that you acknowledge reality and accept that the event happened. If you do not accept the situation, it might be difficult to let go of resentment and move on.

Practice Forgiveness

Sometimes people do despicable things that make it extremely difficult to forgive because we feel violated and cannot understand why someone would do something so terrible and inhuman, even if we did not provoke them. When someone has hurt you, it is natural to want to get back at them, but in life, you must pick your battles wisely.

Prolonged resentment can lead to chronic stress, which makes you more susceptible to other challenging circumstances like health issues and relationship problems. In turn, this can make you feel even more victimized. Forgiveness is a powerful practice that can help you move forward and take control of your life.

Realize That You Cannot Control How Others Treat You

When learning to forgive, you cannot control how others treat you, and the only thing you can control is how you respond to the situation. Try to change your narrative of the painful experience and reframe it in a positive and empowering way.

Another way you can begin to let go of resentment is to steer clear of people who fan the flames of outrage. If you know that someone is likely to trigger a negative emotional reaction in you, limit the amount of time you spend with them.

Take stock of your life by making a list of:

- things you have control over such as your mindset and actions.

- things you cannot control, but you can influence such as your relationships with other people.

- things you cannot influence and have absolutely no control over, such as past events.

177

Spending time thinking about the past only takes away the joy of living in the present moment.

Avoid Being a People Pleaser

It is a good thing to be warm and welcome to people. You can house-sit for your friend once in a while or pick up a coworker's shift at work while they take care of their personal business. Helping others is a commendable thing to do. It can make you look dependable to people, but it also makes you susceptible to disappointment. You can lend a hand to someone, and when it is your turn to ask for help, they drop you like a hot potato. What then? You will likely end up regretting ever helping them and being bitter toward them.

Be kind to people but be kinder to yourself enough to know that you have a maximum threshold when it comes to what you can do. Set limits, love yourself, and practice self-care.

Communicate More Assertively

When dealing with people, it is crucial to understand that some people aren't aware of how their behavior impacts others. Perhaps it is plain ignorance or a lack of self-awareness. Effective communication requires assertiveness. Being assertive is a sign of self-respect and shows your ability and willingness to stand up for yourself, express your thoughts and feelings, and protect your interests.

Effective communication is not just about delivering a message but also about how you convey the message that matters. Assertive communication involves being straightforward while maintaining respect for the other person. It is an effective way to deliver your message to the person or people you are communicating with.

When you communicate aggressively, sometimes your message may get lost or be resisted as people react more to the tone of your delivery rather than understand the point you are trying to put across.

Assertive communication lets people know your expectations. If you want an apology, you must communicate assertively to the person who wronged you. You can do this by:

- **Using "I" statements to express how you feel about the situation:** For example, "I felt disappointed when you did not show up for our appointment."

- **Listening and validating the other person's response:** For example, "I understand that you have a lot going on in your life at the moment, and you seem quite overwhelmed."

- **Setting boundaries:** For example, "In the future, please let me know if you need to cancel or reschedule our plans."

When you communicate assertively, you are more likely to practice self-regulation and not escalate the issue.

Practice Mindfulness

Most people associate mindfulness with meditation. However, mindfulness goes beyond meditation. It serves as a valuable tool to achieve inner peace.

It involves living in the present moment and keeping your thoughts in check. By practicing mindfulness, you can easily let go of resentment, negativity, and anger, allowing yourself to focus on what truly matters—that is the present.

Write Down Your Thoughts, Feelings, and Emotions

If you constantly find yourself thinking negative thoughts, it might be helpful to write down your thoughts, feelings, and emotions. By observing and recording how you feel, you allow yourself to let go of resentment. This allows you to create space for your thoughts without any distractions interfering. While you may not immediately let go of resentment, recording your feelings can help you better understand their impact on your mental well-being.

When you are aware of your feelings of resentment, you can easily come up with effective strategies to help you release these negative feelings and lean toward forgiveness and acceptance.

Share Your Feelings with Someone You Trust

As humans, we naturally thrive when we interact with others. This holds even when we have difficulties letting go of resentment. Speaking to someone you trust—whether it's a friend, coworker, or family member, about your concerns and the challenges you face is an effective way to gain a fresh perspective and resolve any lingering feelings of resentment.

Naturally, we value how others perceive and think about us. So, it is understandable that we often value other people's perspectives more than our perceptions.

Just as you would support a friend when they are at their lowest, your friends are likely to support you as well.

Letting Go of Resentment Practices

If you are ready to let go of resentment and embrace forgiveness and acceptance, here are a few exercises you can begin with.

Identify the Root Cause of Your Feelings of Resentment

It can be difficult to find healing if you do not know what is broken. The first step to letting go of resentment is identifying where it stems from. One powerful way to achieve this is by talking about your feelings. Sharing your emotions with a friend, trained professional, or trusted family member can free you from the trap of negative emotions and pain.

If, for any reason, you are unable to discuss your feelings, you can write an unsent letter to the person who hurt you or write in your journal. It does not matter how you choose to do it, what truly matters is to identify the source of your resentment.

Use a Meditation App to Reduce Mental Clutter

Often, resentment, anger, and anxiety are emotions that develop as a result of underlying feelings of embarrassment, vulnerability, and pain. Applications like Calm, Insight Timer, Smiling Mind, and Headspace offer guided meditations that can help you shift your attention from negative, disempowering thoughts to focus on the present moment and reduce stressful, distracting thoughts while promoting positivity.

Constantly thinking about a painful experience can leave you feeling overwhelmed. Meditation is an effective tool that can help reduce stress. It can also help you reframe your thoughts about the situation and find an effective way to manage stress levels.

Eliminate Anything Associated with the Experience

Resentment is often triggered by former partners or friends and toxic people who have been a part of our lives. If you can end a toxic relationship, you can certainly let go of the lingering resentment toward the person who has hurt you.

To move on, it is crucial to physically and emotionally distance yourself from the people who cause you pain. You can do this by eliminating anything that reminds you of them and the pain they caused you.

Do not be afraid to get rid of the stuff that serves as a constant reminder of how they treated you unfairly. Get rid of that coffee mug—that you thought was a kind gesture from your emotionally abusive ex or donate that Vince sweater that reminds you of the time your friend betrayed you. Once you have gotten rid of anything that reminds you of a painful experience, surround yourself with positive people who uplift and support you. Build and nurture healthier relationships.

Change Your Perspective

Research conducted by psychologists at the University of California-Berkeley suggests that self-distancing from a situation can gradually reduce intense emotional reactions and intrusive thoughts (Ayduk and Kross, 2010). Self-distancing means stepping back from a situation and looking at it from a distance to gain some perspective. It is about distancing yourself from your egocentric point of view and gaining a broader and more objective point of view. This allows you to analyze the situation without an emotional attachment and gain clarity.

Hold the Grudge in a Positive Way

If you have ever held onto a grudge and secretly wished for revenge, you might find this exercise intriguing. However, it goes beyond merely encouraging you to cling to resentment. Holding grudges with a positive mindset can help you change your view about the situation and make you more forgiving.

Instead of allowing grudges to consume you, try using them as reminders of important emotional landmarks in your life. By doing so, you can draw lessons from these experiences about our values, needs, and priorities. In other words, when you change your mindset and look at holding a grudge in a positive light, you can see your experiences as steppingstones, guiding you toward the direction of forgiveness and a brighter future.

Try Walking in the Other Person's Shoes

Putting yourself in someone else's shoes can give your insight into their perspective. It allows you to understand what they have been through and the motives behind their actions. When you realize that as a human being, you have flaws and make mistakes, you can understand that other people make mistakes too and that they are dealing with their own past traumas. This enhances your ability to empathize and show compassion toward others.

Practicing compassion and empathy plays a crucial role in the process of forgiveness. It makes you understand that the way others behave has more to do with their personal experiences than it does with your actions.

Choose a Positive Mantra

Including mantras in your meditation routine can have a positive impact on your overall health and well-being. One of the reasons why mantras are so effective in different situations is their ability to soothe your mind. Unlike other techniques, mantras focus on promoting acceptance and spiritual awareness.

Incorporating mantras into your regular meditation practice can help you become more present, reducing negative thoughts and at the same time promoting a calm, peaceful state of mind. Sometimes, all it takes is a single word or phrase to make a huge difference in your mental and emotional state of mind. All it takes is to say words like, "release" or "forgive" when feelings of resentment arise. Say this mantra to instantly stop negative emotions when they start creeping into your mind.

The journey from pain to breaking the chains of resentment, finding healing, and a way to move forward can be challenging and confusing, but on the other side is a beautiful, tranquil life that awaits you. So, try not to remain stuck in the past, let go of resentment, practice self-care and self-love, and forgive yourself and those who have hurt you. When you change your perspective on pain and view it as an opportunity to learn from your experiences, you open yourself to growing and experiencing more positivity.

Chapter 11

INVESTING IN YOURSELF: PUTTING YOURSELF FIRST

Believing you are unworthy of love and belonging—that who you are authentically is a sin or is wrong—is deadly. Who you are is beautiful and amazing. –Laverne Cox

Living in a fast-paced world where we are always busy, running from errand to errand can make it difficult to focus on vital things, such as practicing self-care. We often get caught up in our careers—working hard so we can climb the corporate ladder. To add on, we have other responsibilities, such as taking care of loved ones and ensuring that all their needs are met. On top of it all, we have to answer to a boss at work, ensure that work projects are completed on time and that clients are happy. But in the process of taking care of everybody's needs, we often neglect our own needs.

What Is Self-Care?

Self-care is all about taking care of every aspect of your life to improve your overall health and well-being. While it is often associated with taking care of your physical body, self-care is not just about physical well-being but also about nurturing your mental, emotional, and spiritual health. Taking good care of our physical health is important, and it starts with adopting healthy eating habits, engaging in regular exercise, and getting enough sleep. However, self-care goes beyond just taking care of your physical well-being. It extends to nurturing your mind and emotions and gaining a deeper understanding of yourself. It involves engaging in activities that bring you joy and inner peace.

Setting aside time for activities that nourish your spirit can help you replenish your energy reserves and experience true transformation—physically, mentally, and emotionally.

Types of Self-Care

Practicing self-care is a vital part of maintaining your overall well-being. Taking care of yourself gives you a sense of balance and leads to a fulfilling and purposeful life. Incorporating self-care practices into your daily routine has many benefits which include boosting your self-esteem and self-confidence. It can also reduce stress, anxiety, and burnout. Prioritizing self-care is essential not only for your health but also for nurturing healthier interpersonal relationships and a happier life.

By incorporating self-care practices into our daily routine, we can effectively manage chronic illnesses such as cardiovascular and kidney disease, stroke, and incident cognitive impairment (Riegel et al. 2017).

To better understand how you can create a self-care plan and begin taking better care of yourself, let us look at what self-care practice looks like in different aspects of your life.

Physical Self-Care

Physical self-care involves intentionally engaging in activities that improve your physical health. The way you choose to take care of your physical health depends on your lifestyle. For instance, if your job requires you to sit for long hours, taking a coffee break and going for a 15 to 30-minute walk during the day can be a fantastic way to prioritize self-care.

Practicing self-care is about finding what practices work best for you—that fit your lifestyle and finding ways to incorporate them into your daily routine. For example, if you work in construction all day, you might opt for some restorative yoga at the end of your shift as a form of self-care practice.

Whether it is through incorporating regular exercise into your routine, maintaining a balanced diet, or getting enough sleep, there are many ways you can nurture your physical well-being. Perhaps you enjoy dancing or hiking. Or, maybe you are an adrenaline junkie and prefer cliff climbing Engage in any form of activity that makes you feel alive—both physically and mentally.

Physical Self-Care Exercise

- Engage in physical activities such as going for a walk, biking, or taking a fitness class.

- Take a relaxing bubble bath after a long day at work.

- Dance to your favorite song.

- Pamper yourself with a full body massage.

- Get enough rest.

Social Self-Care

We are social creatures, and we thrive when we are connected to others. Therefore, to nurture your relationships, it is important to prioritize social self-care and engage in activities that foster your relationships with others. However, there are times when you may be too busy and end up canceling plans and isolating yourself, precisely when you would benefit most from spending time with loved ones. While it is completely understandable to occasionally decline invitations to social gatherings, it is equally important to make time for social interaction and connect with your social circle.

Having a social life can enhance your sense of happiness and well-being, So, if you have not connected with your loved ones in a while, try the following exercise.

Social Self-Care Exercise

- Schedule a regular phone call with your mom.

- Go on a date with your partner.

- Host a game night with your friends.

- Write a card and mail it to a long-distance friend.

While practicing social self-care involves spending time with and connecting with others, it is crucial to take some time to reflect on your relationships. Are your relationships nurturing and fulfilling? If there is someone, whether it is a friend or family member, who constantly drains your energy, you may want to reevaluate that relationship and possibly separate yourself from the person. A healthy relationship should uplift you and make you feel fulfilled rather than leave you deflated and emotionally drained.

Mental Self-Care

Taking care of your mental well-being involves doing activities that promote a healthy state of mind. Mental health self-care is not about achieving a perfect mental state but about being aware of your thoughts and emotions and doing things that encourage a positive state of mind.

If you often struggle to get up in the morning or find your brain feeling exhausted by the end of a busy day, try and include mental self-care practices in your daily routine.

The following techniques can enhance your overall mental well-being and lead to a healthier, happier you.

Mental Self-Care Practice

- **Use relaxation apps such as Calm, Headspace, Insight Timer, and Smiling Mind regularly:** Incorporating meditation, yoga, muscle relaxation, or breathing exercises in your daily routine can help you refocus and center yourself when life feels overwhelming.

- **Practice gratitude daily:** Remind yourself daily of the things you are thankful for in your life. You can write them down in your journal first thing when you wake up in the morning and right before bedtime.

Journaling can help you reflect on the good that surrounds you daily and help you cultivate a more positive outlook.

- **Participate in creative activities:** Activities such as writing, painting, pottery, knitting, or redesigning your space are a great way to practice mental self-care.

- **Read a book or listen to a podcast:** Reading is a therapeutic exercise. It can reduce stress and prevent cognitive decline. Reading and listening to podcasts can be a great source of knowledge. It can change your outlook on life.

- **Play games:** Games like crossword puzzles, and other brain teasers help exercise your brain and improve your memory.

- **Try something new:** It could be a new hobby or meeting new people. Doing something new can help you get to know yourself and overcome some of your fears. It can also stimulate creativity in you. Traveling to a new place and meeting new people can inspire you to embrace the beauty of life.

- **Engage in physical exercise:** Engaging in physical exercise can improve brain health and your ability to carry out daily activities.

- **Take up a course and upskill:** Learning something new trains your brain to cope with and adapt to different situations and keeps your neural pathways functioning (Rodriguez, 2020).

Besides participating in activities that bring you joy; mental self-care also involves taking care of your thoughts and setting healthy boundaries in your relationships. Setting clear boundaries in your life can improve your communication and help you express your needs and limits to others. When you learn to articulate yourself, you lay the foundation to build healthier relationships.

Also, recognize when you need emotional support. If you need to speak to a professional, reach out to one. Therapy can help you explore your thoughts, feelings, and emotions and find ways to overcome pessimistic thinking while cultivating optimism.

Spiritual Self-Care

Taking care of yourself is something that everyone around you can benefit from, regardless of your religious beliefs or culture. Spiritual self-care involves doing activities that help you connect with and nurture your soul. It is about tapping into your inner spirit and connecting with your true essence.

Depending on your beliefs, spiritual self-care involves doing practices that honor a higher power—be it God, the universe, or whatever you may believe guides you in life.

If you want to feel more centered and grounded in your daily life, try the following spiritual self-care practices.

Spiritual Self-Care Exercise

- **Practice meditation and mindfulness to refocus your thoughts and reduce stress and anxiety:** It can help you focus on the present moment and clear mental clutter when life feels hectic.

- **Spend time in nature:** Hiking is a form of physical exercise that can help you connect with nature and improve your mood and your attention.

- **Listen to inspirational music:** This will uplift your mood.

- **Attend church service or attend virtual spiritual activities:** These help you connect with other people who share your beliefs. This will promote a sense of belonging.

- **Pray:** Connecting with a higher power can be beneficial.

- **Volunteer for a cause you believe in:** If you lack meaning and purpose in life, volunteering at a local church or shelter for the elderly can give you a sense of meaning and purpose.

Emotional Self-Care

Being able to manage your emotions and deal with negative feelings when they arise can positively impact your overall well-being. This is why practicing emotional self-care is essential. It allows you to be proactive rather than reactive to life's situations.

Emotional self-care involves identifying and managing your emotions positively. Investing time and effort into this essential aspect of self-care can promote a greater sense of peace within you.

Investing your time and attention in taking care of your emotional health can:

- help you manage your emotions.

- prevent you from being affected by other people's negative moods.

- help you overcome feelings of shame, guilt, embarrassment, anger, or unworthiness.

Prioritizing emotional self-care and treating yourself kindly is a great way to cultivate healthy coping mechanisms. Practicing mindfulness and identifying your negative patterns, such as negative self-talk, can enhance your awareness. You can start noticing when you are spiraling out of control and change negative, unhealthy habits into positive ones.

Emotional Self-Care Exercises

- **Write down your thoughts, feelings, and emotions in your journal:** Journaling your thoughts can help you clarify your emotions.

- **Talk to a therapist, spiritual mentor, or counselor:** Talking about your feelings can help you process them and find effective ways to manage your emotions.

- **Use positive affirmations or mantras:** Positive affirmations can help you reframe your thoughts about yourself. When you repeat positive statements, you reinforce them, and they end up becoming second nature. This allows you to replace negative self-talk with positive, uplifting statements.

- **Practice meditation:** Meditation can increase your happiness and promote emotional stability.

- **Practice gratitude:** Gratitude enhances empathy and can reduce aggression. It can make you more compassionate toward others.

The Benefits of Practicing Self-Care

Self-care can be defined as the actions we willingly incorporate into our lives that improve our health and well-being. It is more than just staying healthy; it involves adopting healthy ways to cope with stress both in our personal and professional lives.

Practicing self-care daily has tremendous short-term and long-term benefits in all aspects of your life.

Short-Term Benefits

By practicing self-care daily, you can begin to see changes such as:

- **Lower stress levels:** Putting your health first, fulfilling your needs, and getting enough rest can reduce stress levels—leaving you feeling invigorated.

196

- **Enhanced self-worth:** When you practice self-care, your perception of yourself often changes. You begin to love yourself more and see yourself in a different light. This is because as you take better care of yourself, you meet most of your core needs. This, in turn, increases your self-worth because you realize your value.

- **Enhanced sense of belonging:** Practicing social self-care can enhance your sense of belonging. When you spend time socializing with others, you feel energized and gain a sense of purpose, which can positively impact your health and greatly improve your mood.

Long-Term Benefits

While practicing self-care has short-term benefits that can help you get through each day, self-care focuses more on the long-term benefits. These include:

- **Reduced risk of chronic conditions.** Practicing physical and mental self-care conditions can reduce the risk of chronic conditions such as depression, diabetes, and cardiovascular disease.

- **Disease prevention.** Incorporating self-care practices into your daily routine, such as regular workouts, eating healthily, and managing stress, can reduce the risk of heart disease, stroke, and obesity later on in life (Riegel et al. 2017a).

- **Reduced stress levels.** Stress has an impact on every system in your body, and prolonged stress can result in chronic health conditions such as high blood pressure, gastrointestinal disorders, cardiovascular disease, and other chronic health conditions. Practicing self-care can reduce the risk of chronic illnesses and promote better health.

- **Healthier relationships.** When you take care of your needs, you can take better care of others. This can improve your relationships partly because self-care leads to an increased sense of self-esteem and self-worth—a key element in building healthy relationships.

- **Enhanced job satisfaction.** A study on effective ways to improve well-being and reduce burnout found that participants who practiced self-care, mindfulness, and awareness and had social support showed significantly higher job satisfaction. The study found that healthcare professionals showed improved well-being and reduced levels of burnout (Adnan et al., 2022).

- **Less burnout.** Practicing self-care has been found to decrease burnout. Taking care of your body, eating healthily, exercising, and getting enough rest can prevent burnout and improve your overall well-being.

- **Improved quality of life.** Practicing self-care allows you to take better care of your health. This can help you manage health conditions, reduce stress, and give you a greater sense of belonging and, therefore, improve your quality of life.

Developing a Self-Care Practice

To get started with your self-care plan:

- Determine which activities energize you, bring you joy and fulfillment, and give you a sense of balance.

- Start small. Choose one habit you would like to incorporate into your daily routine.

- Foster that habit by practicing it every day.

- Reflect on the events of the day each evening. How do you feel? Do you feel emotionally and physically exhausted? What could be the reason behind your feelings? Do you perhaps need to create a work-life balance? Answering these questions will help you adjust your self-care plan as you progress.

- Add more practices and develop new habits, such as getting up early so you can have time to yourself before you interact with the rest of the world.

- Get support from your loved ones or find a community of like-minded people. Having people to hold you accountable can help you stay inspired. A social group can provide emotional support when you feel overwhelmed and encourage you to continue on your journey of self-love and self-care.

Build a Healthy Physical Foundation

As you practice taking better care of yourself, it is crucial to prioritize and maintain a consistent sleep routine to ensure you get enough rest. Getting seven to nine hours of sleep can improve your physical and mental well-being. Additionally eating a balanced diet that includes fresh fruits and vegetables can support your health and curb diseases.

Remember, It is important to drink enough water and stay hydrated. Hydration plays a key role in maintaining your body's functions. By implementing these exercises and making them a part of your daily routine, you can positively move toward living a healthier and happier lifestyle.

Chapter 12

CULTIVATING POSITIVITY THROUGH MINDFULNESS

*Say something positive, and you'll see
something positive. –Jim Thompson*

Our minds are powerful problem-solving machines, always
ready to find ways to solve problems and explore new
possibilities. However, because of the nature of our minds, it
can be difficult to simply be present and be focused on the
here and now. We often find our minds wandering off to a past
event or thinking about the future. As a result, we end up
overwhelmed by the countless thoughts, stories, and
imaginings that often are not the reality of what is happening
around us.

How do we overcome this and gain more control of our
minds? This is where mindfulness comes in—a tool we can use
to give ourselves a break from our overactive minds.

What Is Mindfulness?

Mindfulness is the practice of intentionally directing your
attention toward the present moment. It involves gently

bringing your awareness to the present moment and focusing on your bodily sensations, which anchor you in the present.

You can practice mindfulness when doing normal meditation sessions or while carrying out your everyday tasks, such as cooking, cleaning, or taking a walk.

When you are not fully present, your mind tends to be preoccupied with responsibilities, thinking about the past or future, and other things that take away your focus from the present moment. This is the natural state of our minds: They think, analyze, and solve problems. This is what the mind is designed for. As a result, it is quite common for us to get lost in our thoughts and be disconnected.

Practicing mindfulness is an effective method of calming your mind and preventing it from wandering. Imagine practicing mindfulness as if you were playing the role of a caring parent within your own mind. Instead of letting your mind run wild with thoughts and emotions, you gently guide its attention toward the present moment.

Sometimes, our minds act like stubborn toddlers—wanting to wander off and get distracted. But by practicing mindfulness regularly and being patient and kind to yourself, you can train your mind to be still and fully present. With constant practice, it is possible for your mind to completely let go of mental clutter that often clouds its judgment and dissolve unhelpful thoughts—allowing you to be fully present and experience your surroundings.

Benefits of Mindfulness, According to Buddha

According to the teachings of Buddhism, having a deeper understanding of our minds and emotions enables us to navigate our actions in a way that leads to wellness and a sense of happiness. This positive state not only benefits us, but it also benefits those around us and enhances our well-being. As we begin to value other people's well-being and happiness, we develop compassion and deeper love.

Practicing mindfulness and cultivating awareness play a crucial role in our lives. These two elements unlock a truly fulfilling and purposeful life.

The main objective of Buddhist mindfulness techniques is to:

- assist us in maintaining our focus and staying alert.

- encourage us to acknowledge and connect with our experiences in a calm and balanced manner.

- help us reach a state of enlightenment.

- enable us to confidently approach life with an open heart.

- to develop empathy toward others and detach ourselves from negative emotional responses. As a result of practicing empathy, our relationships with others and with ourselves are positively impacted.

The Science Behind Mindfulness

Countless studies have documented the numerous advantages of practicing mindfulness. In 1979, John Kabat-Zinn developed the Mindfulness-Based Stress Reduction (MBSR) program at the University of Massachusetts Medical Center (Hoshaw, 2022). Kabat-Zinn developed his program by putting together his studies of Hatha yoga and the valuable teachings from Buddhist principles and his various mentors. Since then, there has been an explosion of research into Mindfulness-Based Stress Reduction (MBSR) and mindfulness in general.

Some of the benefits of practicing mindfulness include:

- **Improved memory:** Studies show that mindfulness can improve our memory abilities. There are times when we forget certain information. This is because of proactive interference—a phenomenon where older memories get in the way of accessing new ones. The results of a study conducted in 2019 suggest that by practicing mindfulness, we can potentially alleviate memory-related difficulties and strengthen cognitive ability (Cherry, 2022a).

- **Improved cognitive ability:** Research indicates that mindfulness can enhance your mental flexibility and sharpen your thinking skills (Cherry, 2022a).

- **Reduced stress, anxiety, and depression symptoms:** Practicing mindfulness can alleviate symptoms of depression, provide relief, and prevent the recurrence of these symptoms in the future.

- **Improved emotional regulation:** Mindfulness can help you become more aware of your feelings and find effective ways to manage them. Emotional regulation is the ability to control your own emotions in any situation.

Mindfulness Practices

To start practicing mindfulness, pay attention to your breathing. Gently direct your focus toward your inhalation and exhalation over and over again. You can practice this anywhere and at any time—whether you are doing household chores, browsing the internet, or even taking your dog for a walk. You can use every moment of your day to be fully engaged in the present.

Techniques for Practicing Mindfulness

To get started:

- Start by bringing your awareness to your breathing. Take a moment to tune into your body and notice the gentle rhythm of your breathing.

- Feel your chest expand and drop as you breathe in and out.

- Pay attention to the sensation of the breath flowing through your nostrils. You may notice that the air feels cool as you take a deep breath in and slightly warmer as you breathe out.

- You may realize your mind begins to wander or your focus is distracted by something in your environment.

205

It is completely natural. Gently shift your focus back to your breath without judging yourself. Remember, the goal here is to be present and focus on your breath.

- Repeat this process again and again.

To practice mindfulness, you can either set a specific time or do it throughout your day.

Other Mindfulness Practices

Mindfulness is an expansive concept that includes a wide range of practices. There are different ways you can incorporate mindfulness into your daily routine. You can try the following techniques to see what works for you.

Mindful Eating

Mindful eating involves paying attention to your eating experiences, your body sensations, and your thoughts and feelings about food. It involves being fully present and aware when you are having a meal—without making any judgment. When you practice mindful eating, you become aware of the food you choose to eat, as well as the physical cues from within yourself and your surroundings. The goal of mindful eating is to understand your eating environment and enhance your meal experience—making it more enjoyable.

Mindful Walking

Mindful walking is about being fully present and aware of your surroundings and how your body feels while taking a walk. To practice mindful walking, choose a specific area you want to focus your attention on; it could be a sensation or feeling, and use it as a reference point to keep your mind from wandering. As you walk, stay connected to the present moment, focusing on your body movement.

Mindful Commuting

Adding mindfulness practices to your daily commute can make your journey more positive and fulfilling. We live in a fast-paced world, and it is easy to get frustrated, whether someone cuts in front of you while you are driving or it's the pressure of meeting deadlines. Instead of rushing through the motions, you can practice mindfulness while you are commuting to work. Pay attention to your thoughts, feelings, and surroundings. By being present, you can easily catch any negative thoughts that arise and release them while focusing on the joy and peace within yourself.

Mindful Coloring

Mindfulness can be practiced in various aspects of our lives. Creative art is another method you can use to enhance your creativity. Taking on art can transport you into a state of mindfulness, the same way meditation does.

Coloring has also been found to have a deep impact on our mental well-being. It takes your attention away from yourself and makes you focus on the present moment. Studies show that adults can control stress and anxiety by engaging in creative art. Results of a study of mindfulness art therapy on female cancer patients concluded that coloring lessened their distress during treatment (*3 Reasons Adult Coloring Can Actually Relax Your Brain,* 2015).

Mindful Therapy

If you are interested in therapy that integrates mindfulness techniques, the good news is that there are different options available to you. Several therapeutic approaches integrate mindfulness practices and can help you achieve inner peace and calm.

Some of these therapies include:

- cognitive behavioral therapy (CBT)

- dialectical behavioral therapy (DBT)

- somatic Experiencing (SE)

- holistic therapy

- ecotherapy

Cognitive Behavioral Therapy

Cognitive behavioral therapy involves identifying and changing negative thoughts and behavior patterns. It is based on the belief that our thoughts, emotions, and actions are all interconnected. Unlike other therapies that focus on the past, cognitive behavioral therapy focuses mainly on how your thoughts and feelings can result in distress. It provides techniques to redirect your thoughts and behavior for your overall well-being.

Cognitive behavioral therapy also promotes self-awareness and reflection, which are crucial aspects of mindfulness. By recognizing and reframing negative thought patterns, you can begin to make positive changes in your life.

Dialectical Behavioral Therapy

Dialectical behavioral therapy (DBT) is similar to cognitive behavioral therapy (CBT). However, DBT focuses more on managing challenging emotions and navigating relationships. It was initially created to help people struggling with borderline personality disorder and suicidal thoughts.

DBT involves techniques that promote resilience when faced with distressing situations, practicing acceptance and mindfulness toward your thoughts and actions, as well as developing skills for emotional regulation and improved interpersonal interactions.

Dialectical behavioral therapy can help you transform your thoughts and behaviors in positive and healthy ways.

Somatic Experiencing

Somatic means related to the body. Somatic Experiencing (SE) is a method that taps into the powerful connection between your mind and body to help with both physical and psychological symptoms. The somatic experience was developed by psychotherapist Peter Levine. It is built on the understanding that stress and trauma can harm the nervous system. This approach involves paying attention to your bodily sensations as a way to address and release lingering trauma that may reside inside of you. By recognizing and working with these sensations, you can experience healing and restore balance within yourself.

Holistic Therapy

Using holistic therapy to achieve effective results requires you to take into account your entire personal experiences, beliefs, and cultural background. Instead of focusing solely on one specific issue or area of your life, holistic therapy requires you to consider all aspects of your life so you can receive comprehensive care.

When using holistic therapy, your therapist may integrate various therapies like reiki, breathing exercises, and hypnosis to enhance your overall well-being.

Ecotherapy

Ecotherapy is a practice that fosters a deep connection with our environment. It allows us to recognize the interdependence of all living beings. When you practice ecotherapy, you not only nurture your relationship with nature but also cultivate a greater sense of well-being within yourself. Whether it is feeling the gentle breeze on your skin, admiring the vibrant colors of a sunset, or doing gardening, ecotherapy can connect you to the natural world and rejuvenate your spirit.

Regardless of the techniques you decide to use, the important thing is to incorporate mindfulness practices into your daily life in a way that resonates with you and brings you joy and fulfillment.

Relaxation Exercise to Relieve Tension

1. Start by getting into a comfortable position. You can lie down or sit.

2. Relax your entire body, take a deep breath through the nose, and slowly exhale through the mouth. Repeat this exercise five times.

3. Next, point your toes upward. Hold, and then release.

4. Point your toes downward. Hold, then release.

5. Then, squeeze your calf muscles and release.

6. Next, rotate your knees inward—toward each other. Hold, then release.

7. Tighten your thigh muscles. Hold, then release.

8. Tightly roll your hands into fists. Pause, and then release.

9. Engage your arm muscles. Hold, then release.

10. Squeeze your buttocks. Pause, then release.

11. Squeeze your abdominal muscles. Hold, and then release.

12. Breathe in and tighten your chest. Hold, then slowly exhale and release.

13. Raise your shoulders to your ears. Pause, then release.

14. Press your lips together. Hold, then release.

15. Open your jaw as wide as you can. Hold, then release.

16. With your eyes closed, scrunch your face, pause, then release.

17. Lastly, raise your eyebrows. Hold, then release.

Despite its seemingly contradictory name, mindfulness is a practice that can help you clear your mental clutter. It is an effective approach that you can easily incorporate into your daily routine regardless of background or circumstances. By practicing mindfulness regularly, you can enhance your experience of the present moment and live a more vibrant and fulfilling life.

Appreciation for life's precious gifts can change your outlook and help you cultivate more positivity in your life. So, embrace this journey of personal growth, develop a zest for life, and be mindful of the blessings that surround you.

CONCLUSION

*Do not set aside your happiness. Do not wait to
be happy in the future. The best time to be
happy is always now. — Roy T. Bennett*

You are probably familiar with your physical appearance because you take time each day to gaze into your bathroom mirror while brushing your teeth and getting ready for work. But how often do you look inward to familiarize yourself with your inner self?

We often undermine the power of self-reflection because we are more focused on the physical world than we are on the internal world. We say we desire change in our lives, and each year, we set goals for ourselves, but at the end of the year, we still feel discontent with our results. Life just doesn't feel fulfilling at all, and you ask yourself, "What is my purpose on earth? Surely, there has to be more to life than this."

Perhaps this is a question that has been hovering over your mind for a while, and you feel like life is happening to you. I can guarantee you that you are not alone. No one has their life completely figured out. This is because life is a journey. Sometimes we take a different route that we have never traveled before, and somehow, we find ourselves lost along the way.

Self-reflection is a crucial part of this journey. However, the crux of it is understanding your inner workings as well as your outer form and integrating the two parts to form a whole and complete version of yourself. Through practicing self-reflection, you understand who you are and why you think and behave the way you do, as well. are. Self-reflection is a form of personal evaluation that gives you a better understanding of who you are and what motivates you so you can make changes in your life. To achieve personal growth, you should spend time in personal reflection. This will help you get to know yourself better and build a relationship with yourself. Ultimately, when you understand who you are now, where you're at, and who you'd like to become, you can easily identify the steps you need to take to get to where you want to be.

Reflecting on your behaviors and the thoughts you generate in your mind in response to your experiences allows you to see what you need to improve on. For example, if you were a bit irritable with a coworker. Through self-reflection, you may realize that your behavior does not align with your values and that this is not how you would wish to be treated therefore, you will not treat others in that manner. This can help you adjust your behaviors to align with who you are and help you live an authentic life.

Developing a positive mindset can help you address behaviors that are not in alignment with your values and who you are becoming. It can teach you accountability. When you understand that actions have consequences, you can begin your journey of reframing your thinking processes and cultivating optimism.

Cultivating a growth mindset can help you recognize that you are capable of changing your circumstances. During the process of transforming your thinking patterns, you discover that you have strengths and abilities that you have not tapped into yet. The good news is that your abilities and positive qualities are not static; you can change them internally and externally.

What do you want to achieve in life? Inner peace? Career success or academic excellence? Or do you want to build more meaningful relationships? Recognizing your capacity for personal growth makes you accountable for your life. You can take charge and choose the direction you want to take based on the goals you set for yourself. Developing a growth mindset can open up new opportunities for you that you may have previously overlooked because of a pessimistic attitude.

While optimism involves cultivating a positive outlook, it does not mean you should always look through rose-colored glasses and not be realistic about the challenges of life. But it is about looking for the silver lining and identifying opportunities in every situation—rather than being fixated on the bad aspects of your life. It is being confident that everything will work out for the best and expecting positive outcomes.

Sometimes, you may not get the results you expected, even after putting so much effort into transforming your life. However, when you maintain a positive attitude, you will realize that failure is part of the process of learning. Babies would not learn to walk if they did not fall and bruise their tiny knees time and again. But babies do not give up when they face challenges. They wobble and fall so many times when learning to walk, but they persist and before you know it, they have developed their muscles and started running on their own. There's a great lesson here for all of us, and that is to never give up in the face of adversity. When you do not achieve your desired outcomes, be gentle with yourself. Like learning any other skill, developing a positive mindset takes time and patience. When you make a mistake, practice self-compassion and self-love. The goal here is not to achieve perfection but to reframe your thinking patterns and develop a new way of thinking that supports your dreams.

Practicing self-compassion makes you realize and accept that mistakes are part of the human experience. When you are compassionate with yourself, you do not dwell on your mistakes or beat yourself up; instead, you find creative ways to solve challenges and learn from the experience.

Self-compassion comprises of:

- **Self-kindness:** Being warm and understanding toward yourself when you face a setback or feel inadequate, rather than criticizing and judging yourself.

- **Common humanity:** Recognizing that you are not alone in your struggles and that your suffering and failures are all part of the shared human experience.

- **Mindfulness:** Being fully present. Paying attention to the present moment, and accepting your thoughts, feelings, and environment.

When you practice self-kindness, you recognize that no one is perfect and that we all have flaws, but you can still love and embrace yourself even when things go wrong. No matter your circumstances, you should always treat yourself like you would a friend—being mindful of who you are and practicing self-acceptance. Part of developing a positive mindset involves building a relationship with yourself. Discover your best qualities and natural talents and utilize them to create the life you envision for yourself.

While it may be beneficial to acknowledge your weaknesses, try not to focus on them. Instead, focus on your strengths. If there is something that you are good at that will enhance your life, then pursue it all without reservation. Take massive action and work toward achieving the goals you set for yourself. If your goal is to be more present and achieve inner peace, then incorporate mindfulness and meditation into your daily routine. This will help you develop new habits that support your goal and can help you accomplish it. When you achieve your goals, your self-confidence is enhanced, and you believe in your strengths and abilities. This can promote an attitude of gratitude, and the more you practice gratitude the more you will attract blessings to be thankful for.

Lastly, when you start doing the inner work, remember that not everyone is on a personal growth journey. There will be people who will say or do things that will hurt you—whether it's a loved one, a coworker, or a stranger. Some people will intentionally try to hurt you, while others will do it unconsciously. Learning to forgive people is the best thing you can do for yourself. And yes, I know that forgiveness is not the easiest thing to do, but forgiving someone releases the emotional hold they have over you. You liberate yourself when you forgive your offender instead of harboring resentment.

While resentment may rear its head every once in a while, acknowledge your feelings and process them constructively. This will help you find the courage to move on from painful experiences.

217

To experience positivity in your relationships, surround yourself with optimistic people. Always choose peace over strife and start building and nurturing healthier relationships.

In closing, I'd like to commend you for your courage in embarking on this journey of growth and self-improvement. Sometimes, we do not realize how our mindset impacts our lives. However, when you realize that you have positive qualities, natural gifts, and talents that you have not tapped into yet, you develop a zest for life and a desire to acquire knowledge on how you can be the best version of yourself. I hope that the strategies and exercises mentioned in this book will enhance your optimism and help you to grow.

Maintaining a positive outlook is not always an easy task, but it is well worth striving for. While you cannot control your outcomes in life, you can control how you react to your circumstances. Be bold and courageous enough to follow your dreams.

As Roy T. Bennet once said, "It's only after you've stepped outside your comfort zone that you begin to change, grow, and transform." (Bennet, n.d.)

Wow! You've made it through the journey! You've learned how to grow a positive mindset. Instead of feeling disempowered, you can change how you view what you're going through—and it all starts with developing a positive mindset.

If you are looking for a resource to recommend to people, this book can inspire you to live positively and with the confidence you need to accomplish your goals.

By sharing your thoughts about this book on Amazon, you are not just writing a review. You are lighting the way for others to develop their positive mindset. Your opinion matters to us, and we kindly request a few moments of your time to leave a review.

To leave a review on Amazon

   * Grab your device: open the Amazon app
   * Open your camera app
   * Point your mobile device at the QR code below
   * The review page will appear in your web browser

Thank you!

Your review means the world to us. It's like passing on a secret map to treasure. This book comes to life when you share what you have learned.

You are playing a big part in keeping this circle of learning alive. Your voice matters. By leaving your review, you are helping countless others like you who are eager to transform their lives.

REFERENCES

Adnan, N. B. B., Dafny, H. A., Baldwin, C., Jakimowitz, S., Chalmers, D., Aroury, A. M. A., & Chamberlain, D. (2022). What are the solutions for well-being and burn-out for healthcare professionals? an umbrella realist review of learnings of individual-focused interventions for critical care. *BMJ Open, 12*(9), e060973. https://doi.org/10.1136/bmjopen-2022-060973

Adoring Creations. (2019, May 10). *90-day sprint method for crushing your goals | fluster buster*. Fluster Buster. https://flusterbuster.com/90-day-sprint.html#:~:text=Have%20you%20ever%20heard%20of%20a%2090%20day

Agathangelou, F. (2015, October 13). *How to identify your good qualities when you feel worthless*. Healthy Place. https://www.healthyplace.com/blogs/buildingselfesteem/2015/10/identifying-your-good-qualities-when-you-believe-youre-worthless

Ashley, S. (2020, August 14). *8 letting go of resentment exercises so you can stop holding that grudge & move on with your life*. PureWow. https://www.purewow.com/wellness/letting-go-of-resentment-exercises

Ayduk, Ö., & Kross, E. (2010). From a distance: implications of spontaneous self-distancing for adaptive self-reflection. *Journal of Personality and Social Psychology*, 98(5), 809–829. https://doi.org/10.1037/a0019205

Barker, W. (2017, June 5). *9 basic emotional needs everyone has & how to meet them*. Mindbodygreen. https://www.mindbodygreen.com/articles/9-emotional-needs-according-to-maslow-s-hierarchy

Bennet, R. T. (n.d.). *Roy T. Bennett quotes*. Goodreads. https://www.goodreads.com/quotes/7708835-it-s-only-after-you-ve-stepped-outside-your-comfort-zone-that

Berns-Zare, I. (2019, May 7). *3 ways to leverage your strengths and increase happiness*. Psychology Today. https://www.psychologytoday.com/us/blog/flourish-and-thrive/201905/3-ways-leverage-your-strengths-and-increase-happiness

Bloom, S. (2014). *7 reasons why helping others will make you live a better life*. Dosomethingcool.net. https://dosomethingcool.net/helping-others-life/

Bottaro, A. (2023, December 5). *Self-Care Is a Trendy Buzzword, but What Exactly Is It?* Verywell Health. https://www.verywellhealth.com/what-is-self-care-5212781

Brennan, D. (2021, October 25). *Mental health benefits of journaling*. WebMD. https://www.webmd.com/mental-health/mental-health-benefits-of-journaling

Carter, C. (2008, April 7). *The benefits of optimism*. Greater Good. https://greatergood.berkeley.edu/article/item/the_b enefits_of_optimism

Celestine, N. (2019, March 11). *How to be happy: Is there a secret key to finding true happiness?* Positive Psychology. https://positivepsychology.com/how-to-be-happy/

Chamorro-Garrido, A., Ramírez-Fernández, E., & Ortega-Martínez, A. R. (2021). Autobiographical memory, gratitude, forgiveness and sense of humor: an intervention in older adults. *Frontiers in Psychology, 12*. https://doi.org/10.3389/fpsyg.2021.731319

Cherry, K. (2012, March 5). *Benefits of Positive Thinking for Body and Mind*. Verywell Mind; Verywellmind. https://www.verywellmind.com/benefits-of-positive-thinking-2794767

Cherry, K. (2022a, September 2). *What are the benefits of mindfulness?* Verywell Mind. https://www.verywellmind.com/the-benefits-of-mindfulness-5205137

Cherry, K. (2022b, November 7). *How do psychologists define happiness?* Verywell Mind. https://www.verywellmind.com/what-is-happiness-4869755

Chowdhury, M. R. (2019, April 9). *The Neuroscience of Gratitude and How It Affects Anxiety & Grief*. Positive Psychology. https://positivepsychology.com/neuroscience-of-gratitude/

Christie, N. (2009, December 1). *"each day comes bearing its own gifts. untie the ribbons."—Ruth Ann Schabaker*. Make a Change Blog. https://www.nancychristie.com/makeachange/2009/12/each-day-comes-bearing-its-own-gifts-untie-the-ribbons-ruth-ann-schabaker/

Coley, D. and S. (2021, December 15). *5 ways to use your talent to benefit others*. David and Sharron Coley. https://davidandsharroncoley.com/5-ways-to-use-your-talent-to-benefit-others/

Collingwood, J. (2016, May 17). *Learning about self-image and how we view ourselves*. Psych Central. https://psychcentral.com/lib/learning-about-self-image-and-how-we-view-ourselves

Conlon, C. (2012, August 22). *Why focusing on your strengths is the best philosophy*. Lifehack. https://www.lifehack.org/articles/productivity/why-focusing-on-your-strengths-is-the-best-philosophy.html

Connors, H. (2023, May 12). *Intentional journaling: A guide to journaling with purpose*. The Intentional Habit. https://theintentionhabit.com/intentional-journaling/

Cousin, L., Redwine, L., Bricker, C., Kip, K., & Buck, H. (2020). The Journal of Positive Psychology. *The Journal of Positive Psychology, 16*(3). https://www.tandfonline.com/doi/abs/10.1080/17439760.2020.1716054

Create a Gratitude Practice. (n.d.). In *school of medicine and public health*. Retrieved December 7, 2023, from https://www.fammed.wisc.edu/files/webfm-uploads/documents/outreach/im/handout-GratitudePractice-Final.pdf

Cruz, R. (2023, August 7). *How to stop comparing yourself to others*. Ramsey Solutions. https://www.ramseysolutions.com/personal-growth/how-to-stop-comparing-yourself-to-others

Dalla-Camina, M. (2023, June 23). *How strengths fuel your confidence*. Psychology Today. https://www.psychologytoday.com/us/blog/real-women/202304/how-strengths-fuel-your-confidence

Datta, S. (2023, June 6). *Gratitude is the best attitude for chronic pain patients*. Psychology Today. https://www.psychologytoday.com/us/blog/chronic-pain-diaries/202306/gratitude-is-the-best-attitude-for-chronic-pain-patients

Davis, T. (n.d.). *Positive mindset: 17 ways to develop a happier mind*. The Berkeley Well-Being Institute. https://www.berkeleywellbeing.com/positive-mindset.html

Debara, D. (2022, June 22). *Goal-setting theory: Why it's important, and how to use it at work*. Better Up. https://www.betterup.com/blog/goal-setting-theory

Definition of forgive. (2019). Merriam-Webster. https://www.merriam-webster.com/dictionary/forgive

Definition of goal. (2019). Merriam-Webster. https://www.merriam-webster.com/dictionary/goal

Definition of pessimism. (n.d.). Merriam-Webster. Retrieved December 19, 2023, from https://www.merriam-webster.com/dictionary/pessimism

DiPirro, D. (2019, May 20). *Thought-tinters: 8 things that impact your thinking.* Positively Present. https://positivelypresent.com/2019/05/thought-tinters-8-things-that-impact-your-thinking.html#:~:text=But%20if%20you%E2%80%99re%20short%20on%20time%2C

Eatough, E. (2021a, July 15). *How to set goals and achieve them: 10 strategies for success.* Better Up. https://www.betterup.com/blog/how-to-set-goals-and-achieve-them

Eatough, E. (2021b, September 3). *Learn how to start journaling. it's a ritual worth the time.* BetterUp. https://www.betterup.com/blog/how-to-start-journaling

Fessler, L. (2018, March 26). *"You're no genius": Her father's shutdowns made Angela Duckworth a world expert on grit.* Quartz. https://qz.com/work/1233940/angela-duckworth-explains-grit-is-the-key-to-success-and-self-confidence

Fletcher, J. (2016, May 17). *Positive Thinking: Benefits and How to Practice*. Psych Central. https://psychcentral.com/health/the-power-of-positive-thinking#benefits

Foliage, J. (2023, April 23). *10 flowers that represent responsibility: meaningful blooms*. Foliage Friend. https://foliagefriend.com/flowers-that-represent-responsibility/

Forest, J., & Dubreuil, P. (2014). *From strengths use to work performance: the role of harmonious passion, subjective vitality and concentration.* 261249732_Dubreuil_P_Forest_J_Courcy_F_2014_ From_strengths_use_to_work_performance_The_ro le_of_harmonious_passion_subjective_vitality_and_ concentration_The_Journal_of_Positive_Psychology _1

58 positive character traits | discover your most powerful qualities. (n.d.). True Mydentity. Retrieved November 26, 2023, from https://www.truemydentity.com/pages/positive-character-traits

4 techniques for practicing self-compassion. (2023, June 26). Cleveland Clinic. https://health.clevelandclinic.org/self-compassion

Gandhi, M. (2019). *Mahatma Gandhi quotes*. Goodreads. https://www.goodreads.com/quotes/24499-be-the-change-that-you-wish-to-see-in-the

Gavin, M. (2019). *Optimism for teens*. Kids Health. https://kidshealth.org/en/teens/optimism.html

Get on with it: Getting over someone. (2020, April 20). Clarity Clinic - Chicago. https://www.claritychi.com/blog/get-on-with-it

Gould, W. R. (2023, June 20). *7 different types of bias and how to work through them.* Verywell Mind. https://www.verywellmind.com/signs-of-bias-7501512

Graebner, K. (2021, June 18). *How to practice self-compassion and tame your inner critic.* BetterUp. https://www.betterup.com/blog/self-compassion

Guru, M. (2023, July 30). *How to practice mindfulness while commuting.* Mindfulness-And-Meditation.com. https://mindfulness-and-meditation.com/blog/how-to-practice-mindfulness-while-commuting

Hannah, S. (n.d.). *How to hold a grudge - the podcast.* Sophie Hannah. https://sophiehannah.com/how-to-hold-a-grudge-2/podcast/

Hannah, S. (2020). *How to hold a grudge: from resentment to contentment: the power of grudges to transform your life* (p. 9). Scribner. https://sophiehannah.com/wp-content/uploads/2018/10/Pages-7-15-from-9781473695528-2.pdf (Original work published 2019)

Harvard Health Publishing. (2021, February 12). *4 ways to boost your self-compassion.* Harvard Health. https://www.health.harvard.edu/mental-health/4-ways-to-boost-your-self-compassion

Helping others dampens the effects of everyday stress. (2015). Association for Psychological Science - APS. https://www.psychologicalscience.org/news/releases /helping-others-dampens-the-effects-of-everyday-stress.html

Hendricks, T. (2020, June 6). *Confronting our biases.* Psychology Today. https://www.psychologytoday.com/us/blog/the-pathways-experience/202006/confronting-our-biases

Hodges, T. D. (2005). *The Quest For Strengths* [review of *the quest for strengths*, by J. K. Harter]. https://files.eric.ed.gov/fulltext/EJ685058.pdf

Hoshaw, C. (2022, March 29). *What mindfulness really means and how to practice.* Healthline. https://www.healthline.com/health/mind-body/what-is-mindfulness#benefits

Houston, E. (2019a, April 9). *What is goal setting and how to do it well.* Positive Psychology. https://positivepsychology.com/goal-setting/#google_vignette

Houston, E. (2019b, April 14). *What is mindfulness coloring? + 39 more creative mindfulness art ideas.* PositivePsychology.com. https://positivepsychology.com/mindfulness-coloring-art/

How to practice gratitude. (2019, November 25). Mindful. https://www.mindful.org/an-introduction-to-mindful-gratitude/

Hubbard, E. (2024, January 10). *Elbert Hubbard quote.* BrainyQuote. https://www.brainyquote.com/quotes/elbert_hubbard_122772

Imbastoni, G. (2023, May 5). *Create a personal vision statement and change your life | BetterUp.* Better Up. https://www.betterup.com/blog/create-a-personal-vision-statement

Indeed Editorial Team. (n.d.). *10 career goal ideas and why they're important.* Indeed. Retrieved December 31, 2023, from https://www.indeed.com/career-advice/career-development/career-goals-ideas

Indeed Editorial Team. (2022, June 25). *8 different types of goals you can pursue (with examples).* Indeed Career Guide. https://www.indeed.com/career-advice/career-development/types-of-goals

Indeed Editorial Team. (2023, March 11). *Positive thinking in the workplace: Benefits and tips.* Indeed Career Guide. https://www.indeed.com/career-advice/career-development/positive-thinking-in-your-career

Johnson, J. (2018, August 22). *Hypothalamus: Function, hormones, and disorders.* Medical News Today. https://www.medicalnewstoday.com/articles/312628#function

Krause, N. (2016, August 5). *7 types of goals: The ultimate guide to goal categories.* Develop Good Habits. https://www.developgoodhabits.com/types-of-goals/

Kuyken, W., Byford, S., Taylor, R. S., Watkins, E., Holden, E., White, K., Barrett, B., Byng, R., Evans, A., Mullan, E., & Teasdale, J. D. (2008). Mindfulness-based cognitive therapy to prevent relapse in recurrent depression. *Journal of Consulting and Clinical Psychology*, 76(6), 966–978. https://doi.org/10.1037/a0013786

Lancer, D. (2019, March 17). *Meeting your needs is the key to happiness.* Psych Central. https://psychcentral.com/lib/meeting-your-needs-is-the-key-to-happiness#1

Lawler, M. (2023, March 17). *What is self-care and why is it critical for your health?* Everyday Health. https://www.everydayhealth.com/self-care/

Logan, A. (2022, December 6). *Can expressing gratitude improve health?* Mayo Clinic Health System. https://www.mayoclinichealthsystem.org/hometown-health/speaking-of-health/can-expressing-gratitude-improve-health

Mackbeth, A. (2021, November 22). *4 real ways to value yourself (and why it's so important).* Tracking Happiness. https://www.trackinghappiness.com/how-to-value-yourself/

Maidenberg, M. P. (2020, October 10). *Practicing gratitude is more important now than ever.* Psychology Today. https://www.psychologytoday.com/us/blog/being-your-best-self/202010/practicing-gratitude-is-more-important-now-ever

Malinchoc, M., Offord, K. P., & Colligan, R. C. (1995). PSM-R: Revised optimism-pessimism scale for the MMPI-2 and MMPI. *Journal of Clinical Psychology, 51*(2), 205–214. https://doi.org/10.1002/1097-4679(199503)51:2%3C205::aid-jclp2270510210%3E3.0.co;2-2

Marissa. (2022, March 24). *101 positive thinking quotes for good thoughts & vibes*. A to Zen Life. https://atozenlife.com/positive-thinking-quotes/

Mayo Clinic Staff. (n.d.-a). *How to stop negative self-talk.* Mayo Clinic. Retrieved November 20, 2023, from https://www.mayoclinic.org/healthy-lifestyle/stress-management/in-depth/positive-thinking/art-20043950

Mayo Clinic Staff. (n.d.-b). *Why is it so easy to hold a grudge?* Mayo Clinic. https://www.mayoclinic.org/healthy-lifestyle/adult-health/in-depth/forgiveness/art-20047692

Mayo Clinic Staff. (2017). *Forgiveness: Letting go of grudges and bitterness*. Mayo Clinic. https://www.mayoclinic.org/healthy-lifestyle/adult-health/in-depth/forgiveness/art-20047692

McCraty, R. (2002, January). *The appreciative heart: The psychophysiology of appreciation*. Research Gate. https://www.researchgate.net/publication/232478613_The_Appreciative_Heart_The_Psychophysiology_of_Appreciation

McQuaid, M. (2014, November 14). *Ten reasons to focus on your strengths. Psychology Today Australia.* https://www.psychologytoday.com/au/blog/from-functioning-to-flourishing/201411/ten-reasons-to-focus-on-your-strengths

Mental. (2019). PsychGuides.com. https://www.psychguides.com/mental-health-disorders/

Mental illness - symptoms and causes. (2022, December 13). Mayo Clinic. https://www.mayoclinic.org/diseases-conditions/mental-illness/symptoms-causes/syc-20374968

Mills, B. (2021, May 5). *How does gratitude affect the brain?* Cognitive Vitality. https://www.alzdiscovery.org/cognitive-vitality/blog/how-does-gratitude-affect-the-brain

Mind Tools Content Team. (2022). *Personal SWOT analysis.* Mind Tools. https://www.mindtools.com/aaiakpy/personal-swot-analysis

Mind Tools Content Team. (2023). *MindTools.* Mind Tools. https://www.mindtools.com/a5g2h6s/golden-rules-of-goal-setting

Mindful eating. (2020, September 14). Harvard School of Public Health. https://www.hsph.harvard.edu/nutritionsource/mindful-eating/

Mindful Walking: Stay grounded by walking mindfully. (2022, March 29). Mindfulness. https://mindfulness.com/mindful-living/mindful-walking

Mindworks Team. (2017, July 5). *What Is Buddhist Meditation?* Mindworks Meditation; Mindworks Meditation. https://mindworks.org/blog/what-is-buddhist-meditation/

Mona, B. (2023, October 30). *Toxic positivity: definition, examples and what to say instead.* Forbes Health. https://www.forbes.com/health/mind/toxic-positivity/

Monson, T. S. (2018, January 3). *President Thomas S. Monson quotes.* Church News. https://www.thechurchnews.com/2018/1/3/23213363/president-thomas-s-monson-quotes-highlights-of-a-prophet-s-teachings

Neff, K. D., & Beretvas, S. N. (2013). The role of self-compassion in romantic relationships. *Self and Identity*, *12*(1), 78–98. https://doi.org/10.1080/15298868.2011.639548

New study shows benefits of reliving past events. (2023, July 19). A.r.u. https://www.aru.ac.uk/news/new-study-shows-benefits-of-reliving-past-events

Nguyen, J. (2023, April 17). *How to Use a Mantra for Your Mental Health.* Verywell Mind. https://www.verywellmind.com/mantras-mental-health-benefits-7112640

Nichols, J. (2014, June 19). *Watch: Laverne Cox shares how "it got better."* HuffPost. https://www.huffpost.com/entry/laverne-cox-it-got-better_n_5511230

Niemiec, R. (2019, June 19). *Use your strengths to boost happiness.* Via Institute of Character. https://www.viacharacter.org/topics/articles/use-your-strengths-to-boost-happiness

Ofei, M. (2023, August 3). *What is a minimalist lifestyle? (And what it's not).* Minimalistic Vegan. https://theminimalistvegan.com/what-is-minimalism/

Osteen, J. (n.d.). *Joel Osteen quotes.* Brainy Quote. https://www.brainyquote.com/quotes/joel_osteen_579095

Pamela. (2019, June 12). *Journal with intention.* Journaling Bliss. https://journalingbliss.com/journal-with-intention/

Panda, E. @ H. (2022, February 4). *How to identify and meet your own needs.* Hopeful Panda. https://hopefulpanda.com/identify-and-meet-your-needs/

Panel®, E. (2021, June 11). *Council post: 13 clever "hacks" to adopt a more optimistic mindset.* Forbes. https://www.forbes.com/sites/forbescoachescouncil/2021/06/11/13-clever-hacks-to-adopt-a-more-optimistic-mindset/?sh=1eed90762f43

Parton, D. (n.d.). *Dolly Parton quotes*. BrainyQuote. https://www.brainyquote.com/quotes/dolly_parton_126883

Perry, E. (2022, September 22). *How to focus on yourself and be your own priority*. Better Up. https://www.betterup.com/blog/how-to-focus-on-yourself

Perry, E. (2021, June 27). *Personal goals that work: 20 examples to get started*. Better Up. https://www.betterup.com/blog/personal-goals

Perry, E. (2023a, February 24). *Positive personality traits: Learn to identify and develop them*. Better Up. https://www.betterup.com/blog/positive-personality-traits

Perry, E. (2023b, December 15). *10 wellness goals examples for a healthier life*. Better Up. https://www.betterup.com/blog/wellness-goals

Phillips, A. (2023, November 14). *Growing with gratitude: Boosting confidence and self-esteem*. LinkedIn. https://www.linkedin.com/pulse/growing-gratitude-boosting-confidence-self-esteem-andrena-phillips-rnhke/

Plows, V. (2014, October 5). *Labelling kids: The good, the bad and the ADHD*. The Conversation. https://theconversation.com/labelling-kids-the-good-the-bad-and-the-adhd-31778

Positive Thinking quotes (2948 quotes). (2019). Goodreads. https://www.goodreads.com/quotes/tag/positive-thinking

The power of forgiveness. (2019, May). Harvard Health. https://www.health.harvard.edu/mind-and-mood/the-power-of-forgiveness

Prange-Morgan, C. (2022, November 23). *Why gratitude is good for your health.* Psychology Today. https://www.psychologytoday.com/us/blog/full-catastrophe-parenting/202211/why-gratitude-is-good-your-health

Prendergast, C. (2022, November 30). *Best Meditation Apps Of 2022.* Forbes Health. https://www.forbes.com/health/mind/best-meditation-apps/

Pychyl, T. A. (2013). *Goal progress and happiness.* Psychology Today. https://www.psychologytoday.com/us/blog/dont-delay/200806/goal-progress-and-happiness

A quote from on writing. (n.d.). Goodreads. https://www.goodreads.com/quotes/9209337-you-can-you-should-and-if-you-re-brave-enough-to

Ravishankar, R. A., & Alpaio, K. (2022, August 30). *5 ways to set more achievable goals.* Harvard Business Review. https://hbr.org/2022/08/5-ways-to-set-more-achievable-goals

Raypole, C. (2020a, February 27). *Self-actualization: What it is and how to achieve it.* Healthline. https://www.healthline.com/health/self-actualization

Raypole, C. (2020b, August 18). *Mantra meditation: Benefits, how to try it, and more.* Healthline. https://www.healthline.com/health/mantra-meditation

Raypole, C. (2022, February 28). *How many thoughts do you have per day? And other FAQs.* Healthline. https://www.healthline.com/health/how-many-thoughts-per-day

Rebecca. (2021, February 26). *10 ideas to create sacred space in your home.* Minimalism Made Simple. https://www.minimalismmadesimple.com/home/sacred-space/

Rebecca. (2022, June 13). *10 simple ways to check-in with yourself.* Minimalism Made Simple. https://www.minimalismmadesimple.com/home/check-in-with-yourself/

Regan, S. (2022, August 12). *When forgiveness feels impossible, here's how to move forward.* Mindbodygreen. https://www.mindbodygreen.com/articles/how-to-forgive-someone

Reid, S. (n.d.). *Gratitude: The benefits and how to practice it.* Help Guide. https://www.helpguide.org/articles/mental-health/gratitude.htm

Resentment. (n.d.). *Good Therapy Blog.*
https://www.goodtherapy.org/blog/psychpedia/resen
tment#What%20Is%20Resentment?

Riegel, B., Moser, D. K., Buck, H. G., Dickson, V. V., Dunbar,
S. B., Lee, C. S., Lennie, T. A., Lindenfeld, J., Mitchell,
J. E., Treat-Jacobson, D. J., & Webber, D. E. (2017).
Self-Care for the prevention and management of
cardiovascular disease and stroke. *Journal of the
American Heart Association, 6*(9).
https://doi.org/10.1161/jaha.117.006997

Riopel, L. (2020, February 7). *19 self-image examples &
tools for a positive sense of self.* Positive Psychology.
https://positivepsychology.com/self-image-examples-
activities/#google_vignette

Rivas, K. (2020, November 23). *Finding balance between
meeting your needs vs. others.* Kristin Rivas.
https://kristinrivas.com/finding-balance-between-
meeting-your-needs-vs-others/

Roguska, Z. (2021, October 23). *What Are Basic Human
Needs?* Peep Strategy.
https://peepstrategy.com/what-are-basic-human-
needs/

7 types of self-care & why you need them. (2021, September
6). Health Coach Institute.
https://www.healthcoachinstitute.com/articles/7-
types-of-self-care/

7 ways to boost your health by practicing gratitude. (2023,
November 20). Cleveland Clinic.
https://health.clevelandclinic.org/gratitude-for-

wellness

Schwartz, T., & Porath, C. (2017, December 6). *The power of meeting your employees' needs.* Harvard Business Review. https://hbr.org/2014/06/the-power-of-meeting-your-employees-needs

Scott, E. (n.d.-a). *3 reasons why forgiveness is good for you.* Verywell Mind. https://www.verywellmind.com/the-benefits-of-forgiveness-3144954

Scott, E. (n.d.-b). *The differences between optimists and pessimists.* Verywell Mind. Retrieved December 19, 2023, from https://www.verywellmind.com/the-benefits-of-optimism-3144811#:~:text=Optimism%20is%20a%20mental%2 0attitude%20characterized%20by%20hope

Scott, E. (2019). *Helping others can increase happiness and reduce stress.* Verywell Mind. https://www.verywellmind.com/stress-helping-others-can-increase-happiness-3144890

Scott, E. (2020, October 28). *5 steps to being more of an optimist.* Verywell Mind. https://www.verywellmind.com/become-more-of-an-optimist-3144818#:~:text=The%20key%20to%20optimism%2 0is%20to%20maximize%20your

Scott, S. (2023, January 12). *Mindful commuting: making time for mindfulness during free moments.* Happier Human. https://www.happierhuman.com/mindful-commuting/

Self-compassion - exploring the myths & benefits of self-compassion. (2017, August 3). Mi-Psych | Mindfulness & Clinical Psychology Solutions. https://mi-psych.com.au/the-benefits-of-self-compassion/

Setting goals is the first step in turning the invisible into the visible. (2018, July 15). Good News Network. https://www.goodnewsnetwork.org/tony-robbins-quote-on-goal-setting/

Shah, M. (2022, October 3). *Life isn't about finding yourself. Life is about creating yourself.* SetQuotes. https://www.setquotes.com/life-isnt-about-finding-yourself-life-is-about-creating-yourself/

Shahar, G. (2017, August 9). *The hazards of self-criticism.* Psychology Today. https://www.psychologytoday.com/us/blog/stress-self-and-health/201708/the-hazards-self-criticism#:~:text=Research%20in%20the%20US%2C%20Canada%2C%20Israel%2C%20and%20Europe

Shankar, Preethi, Premavathy, Dinesh, & Preetha S. (2020, October). *Impact of positive thoughts on immunity.* EBSCO Information Services. https://web.s.ebscohost.com/abstract?direct=true&profile=ehost&scope=site&authtype=crawler&jrnl=09739122&AN=148409974&h=hqOLD7liEIIW9XrXey08P17JtTR8TR%2fut3ix%2bztT7B3mgGOeHbIQvsTQUxgQWb2Yi6rkNUkODr0YNPB8snWLTg%3d%3d&crl=c&resultNs=AdminWebAuth&resultLocal=ErrCrlNotAuth&crlhashurl=login.aspx%3fdirect%3dtrue%26pr

ofile%3dehost%26scope%3dsite%26authtype%3dcra
wler%26jrnl%3d09739122%26AN%3d148409974

Sheanoy, P. (2023). *20 goals to set for yourself to further your personal development.* Indeed Career Guide.
https://www.indeed.com/career-advice/career-development/list-of-goals-set-for-yourself

Shermer, M. (2007). Eat, drink and be merry. *Scientific American, 296*(2), 29–29.
https://doi.org/10.1038/scientificamerican0207-29

Shields, B. (n.d.). *Brooke Shields quotes.* Goodreads.
Retrieved January 10, 2024, from
https://www.goodreads.com/author/quotes/62393.B
rooke_Shields

Shokrpour, N., Sheidaie, S., Amirkhani, M., Bazrafkan, L., & Modreki, A. (2021). Effect of positive thinking training on stress, anxiety, depression, and quality of life among hemodialysis patients: a randomized controlled clinical trial. *Journal of Education and Health Promotion, 10,* 225.
https://doi.org/10.4103/jehp.jehp_1120_20

Siedlecka, E., Capper, M. M., & Denson, T. F. (2015). Negative emotional events that people ruminate about feel closer in timenegative emotional events that people ruminate about feel closer in time. *Plos One,* Abstract.
https://journals.plos.org/plosone/article?id=10.1371/journal.pone.0117105

Smak, V. (2017, September 22). *Unlocking the secrets of clutter: how decluttering reduces cortisol levels and transforms your life.* Seedoget. https://www.seedoget.com/blog/unlocking-the-secrets-of-clutter-how-decluttering-reduces-cortisol-levels-and-transforms-your-life#:~:text=Cortisol%2C%20often%20referred%20to%20as%20the%20stress%20hormone%2C

Smookler, E. (2018, June 1). *Look on the bright side?* Mindful. https://www.mindful.org/look-on-the-bright-side/

Solan, M. (2021, July 1). *Thoughts on optimism.* Harvard Health. https://www.health.harvard.edu/mind-and-mood/thoughts-on-optimism

Spratt, B. (n.d.). *7 ways to create a sacred space in your home.* Brandon Spratt. Retrieved December 1, 2023, from https://www.brandonspratt.com/journal/how-to-create-a-sacred-space-in-your-home

Stauner, N. (2023). Personal goal attainment, psychological well-being change, and meaning in life [PDF]. In *Research Gate.* https://www.researchgate.net/publication/261699598_Personal_Goal_Attainment_Psychological_Well-Being_Change_and_Meaning_in_Life

Stevens, M., & Castillo, Beatrice. B. (2019, January 14). *3 simple things you can do right now to win at work.* CNBC. https://www.cnbc.com/2019/01/14/marcus-buckingham-3-scientifically-proven-ways-to-win-at-work.html

Stevens, R. (2018, April 11). *Focusing on your strengths is the key to successful personal development.* Work Brighter. https://workbrighter.co.uk/focusing-on-your-strengths/

Stokes, V. (2020, May 13). *How a life coach taught me to stop comparing myself to others.* Healthline. https://www.healthline.com/health/mental-health/learned-stop-comparing

Stuart, J. (2016, January 12). *Stop trying to fit in and start embracing your true self.* Tiny Buddha. https://tinybuddha.com/blog/stop-trying-to-fit-in-and-start-embracing-your-true-self/

Sutton, J. (2022, January 9). *The fight-or-flight response: everything you need to know.* PositivePsychology.com. https://positivepsychology.com/fight-or-flight-response/

Tello, M. (2019, February 14). *A positive mindset can help your heart.* Harvard Health Blog. https://www.health.harvard.edu/blog/a-positive-mindset-can-help-your-heart-2019021415999

10 keys to happier living. (n.d.). Action for Happiness. Retrieved December 16, 2023, from https://actionforhappiness.org/10-keys/giving

Thesaurus results for intelligent. (n.d.). Merriam-Webster Dictionary. Retrieved November 26, 2023, from https://www.merriam-webster.com/thesaurus/intelligent

3 reasons adult coloring can actually relax your brain. (2015, November 13). Cleveland Clinic. https://health.clevelandclinic.org/3-reasons-adult-coloring-can-actually-relax-brain/

Topor, D. R. (2019, October 16). *If you are happy and you know it... you may live longer.* Harvard Health Blog. https://www.health.harvard.edu/blog/if-you-are-happy-and-you-know-it-you-may-live-longer-2019101618020

Tracy, B. (2022, September 1). *The Power Of Positive Thinking.* Brian Tracy. https://www.briantracy.com/blog/personal-success/positive-thinking/

Tseng, J., & Poppenk, J. (2020). Brain meta-state transitions demarcate thoughts across task contexts exposing the mental noise of trait neuroticism. *Nature Communications, 11*(1), 3480. https://doi.org/10.1038/s41467-020-17255-9

Vanbuskirk, S. (2021, August 19). *The mental health effects of holding a grudge.* Verywell Mind. https://www.verywellmind.com/the-mental-health-effects-of-holding-a-grudge-5176186

Wang, X., & Song, C. (2023). The impact of gratitude interventions on patients with cardiovascular disease: a systematic review. *Frontiers in Psychology, 14.* https://doi.org/10.3389/fpsyg.2023.1243598

Washington, N. (2020, February 4). *Cognitive restructuring: techniques and examples.* Healthline. https://www.healthline.com/health/cognitive-restructuring#self-monitoring

WebMD Editorial Contributors. (2017, February 6). *What is cortisol?* WebMD. https://www.webmd.com/a-to-z-guides/what-is-cortisol#1

Why Is Optimism Important? (26 benefits of optimism). (2022, August 1). Enlightio. https://enlightio.com/why-is-optimism-important-benefits

Wilde, O. (2019). *Oscar Wilde quotes.* Goodreads. https://www.goodreads.com/quotes/19884-be-yourself-everyone-else-is-already-taken

Winfrey, O. (n.d.). *Oprah Winfrey quotes.* Goodreads. Retrieved January 10, 2024, from https://www.goodreads.com/quotes/1264589-know-what-sparks-the-light-in-you-then-use-that

Wooll, M. (2022a, February 7). *Self-criticism and how to overcome it.* BetterUp. https://www.betterup.com/blog/self-criticism

Wooll, M. (2022b, August 5). *10 smart goal examples for your whole life.* Better Up. https://www.betterup.com/blog/smart-goals-examples

Zapata, K. (2020, January 24). *Some Experts Say Minimalism Is the Key to Happiness—But Are You Ready to Purge?* Oprah Daily. https://www.oprahdaily.com/life/a30530266/what-is-a-minimalist-lifestyle/

Zolezzi, A. (2023, June 30). *Gratitude and self-awareness: Benefits of being thankful for your inner life*. Antony Zollezi. https://anthonyzolezzi.com/blog/2023/06/30/gratitude-and-self-awareness-benefits-of-being-thankful-for-your-inner-life/#:~:text=Gratitude%20serves%20as%20a%20catalyst%20for%20self-reflection%20and

Printed in Dunstable, United Kingdom